# FREE AND EQUAL

# FREE AND EQUAL

## A Philosophical Examination
## of Political Values

———

RICHARD NORMAN

OXFORD UNIVERSITY PRESS
1987

Oxford University Press, Walton Street, Oxford OX2 6DP
Oxford New York Toronto
Delhi Bombay Calcutta Madras Karachi
Petaling Jaya Singapore Hong Kong Tokyo
Nairobi Dar es Salaam Cape Town
Melbourne Auckland
and associated companies in
Beirut Berlin Ibadan Nicosia

Oxford is a trade mark of Oxford University Press

Published in the United States
by Oxford University Press, New York

British Library Cataloguing in Publication Data
Norman, Richard
Free and equal : a philosophical examination
of political values.
1. Equality  2. Liberty
I. Title
323.4'01    HM146
ISBN 0–19–827527–7
ISBN 0–19–827526–9 Pbk

Library of Congress Cataloging-in-Publication Data
Norman, Richard (Richard J.)
Free and equal.
Includes index.
1. Liberty.  2. Equality.  I. Title.
JC585.N66  1987    323.44    86–23873
ISBN 0–19–827527–7
ISBN 0–19–827526–9 Pbk

Set by Hope Services, Abingdon, Oxon
Printed in Great Britain
at the University Printing House, Oxford
by David Stanford
Printer to the University

# Preface

AUTHORS' acknowledgements tend to be insufficiently modest. Even the most original ideas are the product not just of individual influences but of a continuing and developing tradition of thought. Certainly the present book is but an attempt to give renewed expression to an enduring political tradition. It is to that tradition above all that I am indebted, and my task has been to restate it and defend it within the current philosophical context. I take pleasure in the thought that the first great statement of social equality is to be found in the words of 'a foolish priest in the county of Kent', John Ball, 'who for his rash words had been three times in the bishop of Canterbury's prison':

My good people, things cannot go well in England, nor ever shall, till everything be made common, and there are neither villeins nor gentlemen, but we shall all be united together, and the lords shall be no greater masters than ourselves.

I do, however, have my own particular debts as well. I have profited from the occasions on which I read versions of chapter 4 to meetings in Canterbury, Cambridge, Brighton, and London. Valuable suggestions were made by the readers who considered the book for Oxford University Press. Special thanks go to Bruce Landesman, with whom I have discussed these matters over a number of years; to Karen Jones and Tony Skillen for their advice on revisions to the original version; and to Sue Macdonald for all her work on the preparation of the typescript.

R.N.

*Canterbury, July 1986*

# Contents

# I

# Introduction: The Politics of Experience

NOT all political disputes are between conflicting political philosophies. Sometimes they are merely technical disagreements about the most effective means of achieving some agreed objective. Confronted with the task of reducing unemployment, for instance, one political party may argue that a reduction in the level of wage demands will encourage investment and thus create more jobs; another may claim that sufficient investment will not be stimulated in this way, and must instead come directly from state revenue. Here the disagreement is simply about the consequences of alternative policies, and it takes place within a framework of shared goals.

Sometimes, however, political disputes do take on a philosophical character. They are then disagreements about the most basic general principles and values. Typically they take the form of conflicts between different political frameworks employing different concepts, or different interpretations of the same concepts. When we engage in the activity of political philosophy, then, our task is to try to sort out these basic concepts—to decide what they mean and how they are to be used. In this book I want to examine two of the concepts which are at the heart of much contemporary political debate—the concepts of 'freedom' and of 'equality'. I shall look at different views of how they are to be understood, what they imply, and whether they represent desirable political values. In doing so I hope to provide an introduction, by example, to the nature of political philosophy.

In identifying political philosophy with the examination of concepts I do not wish to suggest, as philosophers have sometimes seemed to do, that it is simply a matter of elucidating the meanings of words. We cannot arrive at a proper understanding of 'freedom' and 'equality' merely by looking at how people use the words, for popular usage is varied, confused, and often based upon untenable assumptions. We have to try to construct something coherent out of the variety and confusion. We have to examine the factual beliefs, about human nature and human society, which underlie the different interpretations of these concepts. We have to look at their practical implications. To be committed to a particular interpretation of the concepts is to be committed not just to using the relevant words in particular ways; it is to be committed to certain ideals, and to the belief that those ideals can be effectively embodied in working social institutions. We have to examine those beliefs, to consider whether the ideals and the institutions are really feasible.

The various conflicting interpretations of 'freedom' and 'equality' cohere, I think, into two fundamentally opposed political philosophies, identifiable with two long-standing traditions of political thought and action. These philosophies are characterized, on the one hand, by the view that freedom and equality are complementary values and, on the other hand, by the view that they are incompatible values. I want now to introduce these two views by means of extended quotations from two historical exemplars. The first is from a manifesto of the radical movement known as the Diggers, in the English Civil War. In 1649, in *The True Levellers' Standard Advanced*, they declared:

The work we are going about is this, to dig up George Hill and the waste ground thereabouts and to sow corn, and to eat our bread together by the sweat of our brows. And the first reason is this, that we may work in righteousness and lay the foundation of making the earth a common treasury for all, both rich and poor, that everyone that is born in the land may be fed by the earth his mother that brought him forth, according to the reason that rules in the creation. Not enclosing any part into any particular hand, but all as one man working together and feeding together as sons of one father, members of one family; not one lording over another, but all looking upon each other as equals in the creation.[1]

---

[1] Gerrard Winstanley, *The Law of Freedom, and other Writings*, ed. Christopher Hill (Harmondsworth 1973), p. 84.

They continued:

Take notice that England is not a free people till the poor that have no land have a free allowance to dig and labour the commons, and so live as comfortably as the landlords that live in their enclosures. For the people have not laid out their monies and shed their blood that their landlords, the Norman power, should still have its liberty and freedom to rule in tyranny in his lords, landlords, judges, justices, bailiffs and state servants; but that the oppressed might be set free, prison doors opened, and the poor people's hearts comforted by an universal consent of making the earth a common treasury, that they may live together as one house of Israel, united in brotherly love into one spirit; and having a comfortable livelihood in the community of one earth, their mother.[2]

A century later the Scottish philosopher David Hume, in his *Enquiry Concerning the Principles of Morals* (1752), commented on these ideas in the following terms:

the *levellers*, who claimed an equal distribution of property, were a kind of *political* fanatics which arose from the religious species, and more openly avowed their pretensions; as carrying a more plausible appearance, of being practicable in themselves as well as useful to human society. . . .

But historians, and even common sense, may inform us that, however specious these ideas of *perfect* equality may seem, they are really at bottom impracticable; and were they not so, would be extremely *pernicious* to human society. Render possessions ever so equal, men's different degrees of art, care, and industry will immediately break that equality. Or if you check these virtues, you reduce society to the most extreme indigence and, instead of preventing want and beggary in a few, render it unavoidable to the whole community. The most rigorous inquisition, too, is requisite to watch every inequality on its first appearance; and the most severe jurisdiction to punish and redress it. But besides that so much authority must soon degenerate into tyranny and be exerted with great partialities: who can possibly be possessed of it in such a situation as is here supposed? Perfect equality of possessions, destroying all subordination, weakens extremely the authority of magistracy and must reduce all power nearly to a level, as well as property.[3]

---

[2] Ibid., p. 87.
[3] Section III, Part II.

The Diggers appeal both to the ideal of 'freedom' and to the ideal of 'equality', and it is clear that they see the two as very closely linked. What they protest against is the oppression of one section of society by another, and they see this as, almost indistinguishably, both a violation of freedom and a violation of equality. The freedom which they seek is a shared freedom, the freedom of the oppressed from the domination under which they suffer. Hence they consider that it can be achieved only when that domination is replaced by relationships of equality. A central feature of the equality at which they aim is the shared ownership of the earth and its fruits. It is therefore implied that the prevailing inequality and domination consist in the fact that the ownership of these things is at present monopolized by a limited class of people.

Hume, on the other hand, sees equality as the enemy of freedom. He considers that, because individuals differ in their natural talents and abilities, inequality is inevitable. Some people will tend to be more successful than others, and they will therefore tend to occupy various distinct positions in society. The attempt to render them more equal is, because it runs counter to this natural tendency, bound to be coercive. Hume thus thinks of freedom as being left in the undisturbed enjoyment of the particular position in which one finds oneself, and of the life which one makes for oneself in virtue of one's own particular talents and abilities. Unlike the freedom sought by the Diggers, it is primarily a possession of individuals rather than of classes or social groups.

I would suggest that the most fundamental political conflicts of our own day can largely be understood in terms of this same opposition. Though the terms of the debate have changed in some ways, the same two opposed traditions of thought persist. Thus we find, on the one hand, a political party which aspires to liberate individual economic enterprise from the shackles of state control—and if this means that the 'wealth-creators' prosper more than others do, so be it. On the other hand we find another political party claiming that the freedom thus promised is no true freedom, since it leaves large sections of society crushed by poverty and destitution; effective freedom for them means effective communal provision of medical services, education, care for the elderly, and other forms of social welfare. Again two opposed visions of freedom clash with one another.

The attempt to clarify these concepts is, then, not just a matter for idle philosophical speculation. It is also a matter of practical politics. The philosophical conclusions which we reach are likely to have important implications for the day-to-day world of political action.

Before embarking on that philosophical task, however, I want to anticipate a sceptical objection which may be raised right at the outset. It is a scepticism which may be directed against the very use of terms like 'freedom' and 'equality'—for are these not, it may be said, merely fine-sounding words with no real content? It is a scepticism which is, indeed, induced precisely by the contemporary world of practical politics, and by the appeals which are made to such concepts within that political world. How much has been promised in the name of these ideals, and how little has ever been delivered! And when the rulers of two immensely powerful nuclear-armed states warn us that it is necessary to risk destroying the world in defence of freedom, we are understandably inclined to dismiss their talk of 'freedom' as the manic rhetoric of power-crazed politicians. That is an entirely proper reaction, but it may then extend to a quite general scepticism about political ideals.

A more sophisticated variant of this view of political ideals as empty rhetoric can be found in a particular version of the Marxist theory of 'ideology'. The view here is that conflicting uses of terms like 'freedom' and 'equality' simply give expression to the conflicting interests of different classes. There is 'bourgeois' freedom and there is 'proletarian' freedom, but there is no sense in looking for the 'real' nature of 'human' freedom. It cannot be said straightforwardly that this is the view which Marx and Engels themselves took of political ideals and their ideological character, but it is a view which is undoubtedly fostered by some of the things which they wrote. In the *Communist Manifesto*, for example, they consider the allegation that communism would abolish all personal freedom. Their response is that 'The abolition of bourgeois individuality, bourgeois independence, and bourgeois freedom is undoubtedly aimed at. By freedom is meant, under the present bourgeois conditions of production, free trade, free selling and buying.'[4] They then turn on their critics in the following words: 'But don't wrangle with us so long as you apply, to our intended abolition of bourgeois property, the standard of your bourgeois notions of freedom, culture, law, etc. Your very ideas are but the outgrowth of the conditions of your bourgeois production and bourgeois property.'[5]

So far this is at least consistent with the view that there could be a concept of 'freedom' which not only was non-bourgeois, but was not tied to any particular class at all, or to any particular mode of production. However, they seem to reject this possibility when they go on to say:

Does it require deep intuition to comprehend that man's ideas, views and conceptions, in one word, man's consciousness, changes with every change in the conditions of his material existence, in his social relations and in his social life. . . . The ruling ideas of each age have ever been the ideas of its ruling class.[6]

Following this line of thought, we might be led to the view that the clash we have previously been considering between two conflicting interpretations of 'freedom' simply reflects a clash between the interests of conflicting classes. On this view there is no point in asking which interpretation is 'right'; it is simply a matter of deciding with which class one's allegiance lies.

The underlying assumption of this book is that there *is* a real and objective content to the concepts of 'freedom' and 'equality', and that it is a valid intellectual enterprise to try to clarify what these terms really mean. Certainly they are cynically manipulated by politicians; but we rightly object to such manipulation precisely because it distorts the real meaning of the words. Likewise the notion of 'ideology' gets its force from the recognition that ideological concepts are distortions. Of course concepts can reflect class interests, but that makes it all the more imperative that we should examine these concepts critically and try to discern their real character. This is not to say that as intellectuals or philosophers we are

---

[4] *Karl Marx: Selected Writings*, ed. David McLellan (Oxford 1977), p. 233.
[5] Ibid., p. 234.          [6] Ibid., p. 236.

ourselves somehow immune to the influence of class interests, but simply to suggest that our proper task is to try to see beyond those influences, even if we can never entirely do so.

I cannot show in advance that the concepts of 'freedom' and 'equality' have a real and objective content which we can properly aim to identify. That is an assumption which can be vindicated only by the whole argument of the book. What I shall try to show is that political ideals such as 'freedom' and 'equality' have an authentic content just in so far as they are rooted in human experience. They are not merely abstract ideals. They are not the product of pure reason, residing in some timeless realm of transcendent values. They are the product of people's attempts to give expression to their shared, concrete aspirations, to articulate the limitations and frustrations of existing social life and to envisage alternatives to their present condition. Our task is, therefore, to identify those features of human experience which give these ideals their authentic content.

## 2

# Views of Freedom

I BEGIN, then, with the concept of 'freedom', and with a classic treatment of the subject—John Stuart Mill's essay *On Liberty*, published in 1859. In calling it a 'classic' I do not mean to suggest that Mill has said all that needs to be said on the subject. On the contrary, the essay raises more problems than it solves. But that is precisely its strength. Mill, in all his works, was nothing if not an honest writer, sensitive to the complexities and difficulties of his subject-matter, and *On Liberty*, by its very inconsistencies and contradictions, vividly expresses the tensions within the concept of 'freedom' and the conflicting traditions of philosophical thought dealing with the concept.

Mill writes as a philosopher, not as a political propagandist, but he writes from within a specific political context. His thinking about liberty is influenced especially by the movement towards political democracy. He welcomes that development, but he does not share the illusions of those who suppose that the achievement of universal suffrage will be the complete guarantee of freedom. Democratic elections effectively give power not to 'the people' but to a majority of the people, and the power which would then be exercised over minorities could constitute a 'tyranny of the majority' which could destroy freedom as effectively as any autocratic ruler. In the light of these dangers he sets out to defend the value of freedom (in chapters 2 and 3) and to suggest how it can be safeguarded (in chapters 4 and 5). These two tasks, I shall suggest, lead him to espouse two different and conflicting conceptions of freedom.

Why is freedom valuable and important? The core of Mill's answer comes at the beginning of chapter 3. Mill's approach to all moral and social issues is a utilitarian one. He thinks that human actions and social practices can be justified only by their *utility*—that is, by their tendency to produce as much happiness as possible for people in general. But, he adds, 'it must be utility in the largest sense, grounded on the permanent interests of a man as a progressive being' (p. 136).[1] That sentence is left unexplained, but its importance becomes apparent in the course of chapter 3, in passages such as these:

Where, not the person's own character, but the traditions or customs of other people are the rule of conduct, there is wanting one of the principal ingredients of human happiness. . . . The free development of individuality is one of the leading essentials of well-being. . . . It is the privilege and proper condition of a human being, arrived at the maturity of his faculties, to use and interpret experience in his own way. . . . To conform to custom, merely *as* custom, does not educate or develop in him any of the qualities which are the distinctive endowment of a human being. The human faculties of perception, judgment, discriminative feeling, mental activity, and even moral preference, are exercised only in making a choice. . . . Human nature is not a machine to be built after a model, and set to do exactly the work prescribed for it, but a tree, which requires to grow and develop itself on all sides, according to the tendency of the inward forces which make it a living thing. (pp. 185–8)

Mill is claiming that, as human beings, we need freedom in order to live a fully human life. To know what makes for human happiness, you have to know what human beings are like. If we belonged to a different species, we might be content with the pleasures of a cow grazing in the field or a monkey swinging from branch to branch. For a human being, mere physical pleasures are not enough. They may have their appeal, but a life consisting of nothing else would be one which, after a while, we would find boring and frustrating. To achieve human happiness, we have to use to the full our distinctively human capacities. We have to think for ourselves, make our own judgements and our own decisions, drawing on our own experience. In short, if we are to find our lives genuinely rewarding and fulfilling we have to exercise our freedom.

This notion of a fully human life has been a persistent strand in the Western moral tradition.[2] It was first clearly

[1] References are to John Stuart Mill, *Utilitarianism, On Liberty, Essay on Bentham*, ed. Mary Warnock in the Fontana Library (London 1962).

[2] I have discussed it further in Richard Norman, *The Moral Philosophers* (Oxford 1983).

formulated by the Greek philosopher Aristotle (384–322 BC). Like Mill, Aristotle identifies the ultimate good with happiness, but—also like Mill—he thinks that to form a clearer idea of what human happiness consists in, we must look at human nature. In particular, he suggests, we must consider what the function of a human being is. Just as particular classes of human beings, such as builders or shoemakers, have their own distinctive function, so also, he thinks, human beings in general must have a characteristic function. Or again, if particular parts of the body such as the eye or hand or foot each have their proper function, then surely the human being as a whole must likewise have an appropriate function. This is to be ascertained, he thinks, by identifying the distinctive features of human beings which mark them off from all other living species. We share with all other living things the capacities for nutrition and growth. We share with other animals the capacity for sensation. What is unique to human beings is the capacity for reason. This, then, is our distinctive function, and we live a fully human life when we live the life of reason.[3]

For Aristotle, this conclusion has élitist connotations.[4] Though reason is the distinguishing mark of the human species, not all humans possess it to the same degree. Non-Greeks are less capable of employing reason than Greeks, and therefore they are natural slaves. Women are less capable of reasoning than men, and therefore their natural and proper role is to be ruled by men. The political conclusions to which Aristotle is led are therefore very different from Mill's. Mill, too, has sometimes been accused of élitism, but the accusation seems to me to be unjust. Certainly he would reject Aristotle's view of racial and sexual differences. For that matter, he would not employ Aristotle's talk of a human 'function', but what he shares with Aristotle is the ideal of the fully human life. It is his profound conviction that all human beings, unless they are corrupted by circumstances, are capable of living such a life, and his defence of freedom is a defence of a fully human life for all. In a free society, all human beings will be able to live their lives to the full by making their own

---

[3] Aristotle, *Nicomachean Ethics* (often referred to simply as *Ethics*), I, 7.
[4] Aristotle, *Politics*, I, 5.

decisions, exercising their own reason and judgement and employing all their human faculties.

Let us, then, try to formulate clearly and simply the conception of freedom which Mill is employing in chapter 3. It is important to do so, because I shall want to suggest that elsewhere in the essay Mill shifts to a different conception of freedom, and this inconsistency will be central to my overall assessment of Mill's account. For the moment, however, it seems that he is working with a notion of freedom as the ability to make choices and decisions for oneself. We can call this a positive concept of freedom—the significance of that label will shortly become apparent. Essentially the same conception is to be found in chapter 2, where Mill mounts his defence of 'liberty of thought and discussion'. I shall not elaborate here the details of that defence, but the core of Mill's argument is the claim that only by means of free speech can we arrive at the truth. It is, he thinks, through the competition of ideas, through the process of argument and debate and criticism, that competing beliefs can be tested against one another. By testing them in this way we can find out which beliefs best stand up to criticism and therefore best deserve to be accepted. It is therefore essential that all competing beliefs should get a hearing, and that everything should be said for and against them that can be said. Here too, then, Mill seems to me to be operating with a positive notion of freedom, as the active exercise of one's own powers of judgement and decision.

I find a radically different emphasis in chapters 4 and 5. Mill there turns from the question 'Why is freedom valuable?' to the question 'How is freedom to be achieved?' The problem which confronts any philosopher of freedom is that people's freedoms conflict. In the absence of any socially-imposed restraints, the exercise of freedom by strong individuals is liable to crush the freedom of others who are less strong. A 'free-for-all' will not, in practice, produce freedom for all. For the sake of freedom itself, therefore, socially-imposed restraints seem to be needed. How great should these restraints be, then, if they are not to destroy the very freedom they should protect? This is the problem which Mill tackles.

His answer, in chapters 4 and 5, elaborates the basic principle which he has initially stated in chapter 1. Society, he says, should not interfere with the freedom of individuals unless their actions are liable to harm other people. Where people's actions affect only themselves, they should be left free to do as they wish.

Two features of this principle I wish particularly to emphasize. The first is that the concept of freedom is now being given a decidedly more negative cast. When it comes to specifying the practical character of a free society, Mill seems to identify freedom with the negative requirement that people should not be coerced or interfered with. The shift, then, is from the positive concept of freedom as self-determination to the negative concept of freedom as non-interference. Now this may be a perfectly permissible shift—merely a change of emphasis from one aspect of freedom to another. Alternatively it may be a serious inconsistency. It may be that Mill is torn between two incompatible concepts of freedom. Certainly the shift is a striking one. In chapters 2 and 3 we are presented with this magnificent vision of a world in which human beings are able to use to the full their powers of reason and judgement to shape their own lives. But when, in chapters 4 and 5, we turn to consider the kinds of social arrangements which are required in order to realize this vision, we are told simply that people should be left alone. At the very best, there seems to be some disparity between the two conceptions.

The second feature of Mill's principle to which I want to draw attention is that it is framed in terms of a fundamental opposition between 'society' and 'the individual'. The principle draws a distinction 'between the part of a person's life which concerns only himself, and that which concerns others' (p. 210). The ground has been prepared for this distinction at the very beginning of the essay, since Mill assumes from the outset a more fundamental distinction between, on the one hand, freedom as something essentially enjoyed by individuals and, on the other hand, society as the source of restrictions on this freedom. We have seen that his account is coloured by his sense of the danger posed by 'the tyranny of the majority'. This danger is threatened 'when society is itself the tyrant—society collectively over the separate individuals who compose it' (p. 129). Consequently, when at the beginning of chapter 4 he asks 'What, then, is the rightful limit to the sovereignty of the individual over himself? Where does the authority of society begin? How much of human life should be assigned to individuality, and how much to society?' the answer looks obvious: 'Each will receive its proper share, if each has that which more particularly concerns it. To individuality should belong the part of life in which it is chiefly the individual that is interested; to society, the part which chiefly interests society.' (p. 205).

As a solution to the problem of the scope and limits of freedom, however, this answer is less self-evident than it looks. It appears obvious only because the problem has already been posed in terms of the opposition between the individual and society. I therefore want to look more closely at these distinctions—at the distinction between actions which concern oneself and actions which concern others, and then at the underlying distinction between the individual and society. How real are the divisions?

First a word of clarification. Mill himself seems uncertain about the exact nature of the distinction he wants to draw between two classes of actions. One version, we have seen, describes the two classes as consisting in the part of a person's conduct which 'concerns others' and the part which 'merely concerns himself' (pp. 135, 210). This is hardly a satisfactory way of putting it, for the phrase 'concerns others' is altogether too vague. Consider the very first example to which Mill applies his principle—that of religious prohibitions on certain kinds of food, such as the Islamic ban on the eating of pork. Mill says that if non-Moslems eat pork, this is a matter of their 'personal tastes and self-regarding concerns'— yet surely such actions on the part of non-Moslems could also reasonably be said to 'concern' Moslems. As Mill himself says, it offends them and arouses in them a feeling of disgust. And in general, any action of which a certain group of people disapprove could, in some sense, be said to 'concern' those people. Mill's discussion, however, strongly suggests that he would not see this as any ground for restricting the freedom to perform such actions. The terms 'concern others' and 'concern oneself' do not, then, seem to be the right ones for marking the distinction which Mill wants to make. The same goes for the formulation in terms of 'conduct which affects only himself' and conduct which 'affects others' (p. 137). The expression which captures Mill's real meaning more effectively is the distinction between actions which concern or affect the *interests* of other people and those which do not (pp. 136, 206)—or better still, between those which do and those which do not affect *prejudicially* the interests of others. It does not matter whether our actions affect other people in some way or other, provided we do not act contrary to other people's interests. In simpler terms, the division is between actions which do or do not harm other people (p. 135), and we shall best do justice to Mill's position if we take that to be his meaning.

Notice also that Mill is not saying that *all* actions which harm other people should be prohibited. That would be ludicrous. There are, alas, innumerable ways in which in our daily lives we inflict petty injuries on others, through thoughtless or unkind words or deeds. If social restraints were to be placed on all these, the machinery of coercion would be hopelessly overburdened. Mill's real position is stated thus: 'As soon as any part of a person's conduct affects prejudicially the interests of others, society has jurisdiction over it, and the question whether the general welfare will or will not be promoted by interfering with it, becomes open to discussion' (p. 205; see also p. 226). In other words, when actions harm other people, the question arises whether they should be prohibited. In some cases the appropriate response will simply be one of disapproval. In other cases, where actions inflict serious harm on others, the appropriate response will be one of active interference to prohibit or punish such actions. And what the appropriate response is must be settled, like all moral and social questions, by a utilitarian calculation—by assessing how much good or harm will be done by the various possible responses.

This, then, is Mill's position, and we must now consider whether it stands up to examination. Can the distinction between the two classes of actions, even on its most plausible interpretation, be sustained? I want to test it against some examples. Mill provides his own, but it may be interesting to look at some modern examples—cases where Mill's position seems to have an initial plausibility. Consider then the following.

1. Changes in the law in recent years have made it compulsory for people riding in the front seats of cars to wear safety belts, and for riders of motor-cycles to wear crash-helmets. These regulations are intended to reduce the risk of serious injury, but they have been resented in some quarters. The response of some people has been 'Why shouldn't I run that risk if I choose to do so? It's up to me. It's my own life that I'm risking, not anyone else's, and the law shouldn't force me to be cautious if I don't want to be.' This looks like a response which would have Mill's blessing. The law is manifestly intended to prevent people harming themselves, not to prevent them harming others. But is the distinction in fact so clear-cut? If people do incur serious injury as a result of not wearing a seat-belt or a crash-helmet, they will need medical attention and use scarce medical resources which could otherwise have been used to treat others suffering from less avoidable injuries. In running the risk of injury to oneself, therefore, it seems that one is inevitably also running the risk of harming others.

2. Laws at present prohibit the use of various hallucinatory drugs. Opposition to these laws has in part taken the form of questioning whether some of these drugs (for example, LSD, or marijuana) are really harmful. But even in the case of drugs such as heroin, which unquestionably lead to drastic physical deterioration, some people would argue that the law should not prevent people destroying themselves if that is what they choose to do. Again the response seems to have Mill on its side, but again there are problems with such a response. One problem, which I simply note here without discussion, is that the drug addict, just because he or she is an addict, can hardly be said to have freely chosen his or her own destruction. The second problem is akin to that in the previous example. The drug addict becomes a drain on his or her society, using up medical facilities and becoming incapable of making any contribution to the society or playing any positive part in it. So the addict's own individual well-being seems to be tied up with that of his or her society, in

ways which make it difficult to apply Mill's principle.

3. There are laws which prohibit or restrict the sale of pornographic material. Setting aside the fact that these laws do not seem to be particularly effective, one might also object to them on the grounds that they constitute an undue interference with the freedom of the individual. One might make this objection even while accepting that pornography panders to corrupt and debased sexual tastes, and insist that so long as the consumer of pornography confines his or her tastes to his or her own private life and makes no attempt to impose them on others, the law has no business to interfere. Again, however, further reflection may lead us to ask whether the supposedly private sphere is in fact purely private. There is such a thing as a general sexual culture, a climate of habits and attitudes and opinions, and corrupt and debased private activities will, by their very existence, contribute to a corrupt and debased culture. This will in turn find expression in more publicly observable ways, in a deterioration in the quality of people's sexual relationships. The mutual respect and love which many would feel ought to characterize such relationships may become more difficult to sustain in an unsympathetic moral climate. Here too, then, supposedly private actions seem to have inescapable implications for the public world.

Mill is aware of these difficulties, and attempts to deal with them by distinguishing between direct and indirect effects on others. After the initial statement of his principle in chapter 1, he comments on the phrase 'conduct which affects only himself': 'When I say only himself, I mean directly, and in the first instance; for whatever affects himself, may affect others through himself; and the objection which may be grounded on this contingency, will receive consideration in the sequel' (p. 137). The relevant 'sequel' comes in chapter 4, where he envisages the objection: 'No person is an entirely isolated being; it is impossible for a person to do anything seriously or permanently hurtful to himself, without mischief reaching at least to his near connections, and often far beyond them' (pp. 210–1). He considers cases, analogous to my modern examples, such as a man who spends all his money on drink and consequently is unable to pay his debts or to support his family. The man could be 'deservedly reprobated' and 'justly punished', according to Mill, 'for the breach of duty to his family or creditors', but not for being drunk or squandering his money. In themselves these actions are his own concern. Mill's general response to the objection, then, is:

Whenever, in short, there is a definite damage, or a definite risk of damage, either to an individual or to the public, the case is taken out of the province of liberty, and placed in that of morality or law. But with regard to the merely contingent, or, as it may be called, constructive injury which a person causes to society, by conduct which neither violates any specific duty to the public, nor occasions perceptible hurt to any assignable individual except himself; the inconvenience is one which society can afford to bear, for the sake of the greater good of human freedom. (p. 213)

Mill would therefore presumably say that the driver without a seat-belt who risks using up valuable medical resources, or the drug-addict who becomes a drain on society, are causing only indirect harm to others and should therefore not be legally prohibited from driving without a seat-belt or using drugs. The harm is not a specifiable and identifiable harm to a specifiable and identifiable person or group of people. As such, Mill seems to imply, the harm is less important; it is 'one which society can afford to bear'. It is not at all clear, however, why this implication should be thought to follow. Why should a harm be any less, or less important, because it is indirect? If my refusal to wear a seat-belt lands me in hospital, I am adding to the waiting-list for hospital beds, and the result is that other people will suffer or die because the hospital cannot take them in time. Of course I cannot specify *who* will suffer or die as a result of my action, but *someone* will, and their suffering or death is not less important just because I cannot say whose it is.

If Mill recognizes that 'no person is an entirely isolated being', and that any harm to oneself is always indirectly a harm to others too, he ought also to recognize that this undermines his principle. Indirect harms are no less important for being indirect. They cannot be simply discounted as a minor complication for the principle. Their significance, rather, is that the intended distinction between actions which harm others and actions which affect only one's own interests cannot effectively be drawn.

There are philosophers who would say that this is no accident. The difficulty of drawing a clear line between the public and the private sphere is not merely, they would say, an unfortunate reflection of the complexity of human life. It reflects the inadequacy of a whole way of thinking, one which assumes an antithesis between 'the individual' on the one hand and 'society' on the other. Mill, we saw, takes this antithesis for granted. Other philosophers, however, have questioned it, and have found it untenable and misleading. The individual, they say, *is* the social being.

This line of thought has a long history. It was espoused by the two great social philosophers of antiquity, Plato and Aristotle.[5] The latter has, in his *Politics*, given it its classic formulation: 'man is by nature a politikon zoon'—a political animal, a social animal, literally a 'city-state' animal.[6] In more recent times this view has been central to the philosophical tradition stemming from the German philosopher Hegel, and, in virtue of Hegel's influence on Marx, has also been central to Marxism.[7] A good example, exhibiting a clarity and vigour of style rare among Hegelian philosophers, is the work of F. H. Bradley, one of the group of British Hegelians active at Oxford in the latter part of the nineteenth century. Bradley's book *Ethical Studies* contains a chapter called 'My Station and its Duties' which is an explicit attack on individualism, and it is obvious that Bradley has Mill in mind as the principal target. Whereas Mill identifies the fully human life, the full development of one's human capacities, with the pursuit of individuality, Bradley argues, on the contrary, that self-realization is to be found in the fulfilment of one's roles and duties in society. The individual outside society is nothing, an impossibility; 'what we call an individual man is what he is because of and by virtue of community' (p. 166).[8]

---

[5] See, for example, Plato, *The Republic*, II, 369B–371E.

[6] Aristotle, *Politics*, I, 2.

[7] See, for example, G. W. F. Hegel, *The Philosophy of Right*, trans. T. M. Knox (Oxford 1952), paras. 142–57. For a very clear exposition, see Peter Singer, *Hegel* (Oxford 1983), ch. 3. For Marx, see for example K. Marx and F. Engels, *The German Ideology*, Part 1 (selections in McLellan, *Karl Marx*, p. 159 ff.), and the opening pages of the Introduction to the *Grundrisse* (McLellan, pp. 345–7).

[8] References are to F. H. Bradley, *Ethical Studies*, 2nd edn. (Oxford 1927)

The growing child, argues Bradley, cannot acquire a way of life, cannot even acquire a conception of itself and of its own needs and aspirations, except by imbibing the habits and customs of its own community;

he does not even think of his separate self, he grows with his world, his mind fills and orders itself; and when he can separate himself from that world, and know himself apart from it, then by that time his self, the object of his self-consciousness, is penetrated, infected, characterized by the existence of others. Its content implies in every fibre relations of community. (p. 172)

Bradley emphasizes especially that one acquires one's *moral* identity from one's society. As we learn a language, we acquire moral concepts and values—notions such as honesty, integrity, justice, loyalty, and fidelity—and it is in terms of these that we do our moral thinking. One may in due course come to criticize features of one's own society and its moral code, but one can do so only by using the moral concepts which have themselves been acquired from that society.

How does this affect our assessment of Mill? Something like Bradley's position is invoked (though not by name) in a provocative lecture on 'The Enforcement of Morals' given by Lord Devlin, a former high court judge, in 1959. The lecture is directed not primarily at Mill, but at the Wolfenden Report on Homosexual Offences and Prostitution which appeared in 1957. The Report recommended important changes in the law: homosexual behaviour between consenting adults in private should no longer be a criminal offence; soliciting by prostitutes, on the other hand, should be made illegal. It argued for these recommendations by appealing to a particular view of the function of the criminal law:

its function, as we see it, is to preserve public order and decency, to protect the citizen from what is offensive or injurious, and to provide sufficient safeguards against exploitation and corruption of others. . . . It is not, in our view, the function of the law to intervene in the private lives of citizens . . . there must remain a realm of private morality and immorality which is, in brief and crude terms, not the law's business. (quoted by Devlin, pp. 2–3)[9]

---

[9] References are to Patrick Devlin, *The Enforcement of Morals* (Oxford 1965).

This distinction between public order and decency and the protection of the citizen on the one hand, and private morality and immorality on the other, is not Mill's distinction. Nevertheless, it clearly belongs to the same family of ideas, and it is against this influential modern version of the doctrine that Devlin directs his attack. Like Bradley, he argues that questions of morality and immorality cannot, by their very nature, be purely private concerns. Morality is essentially a social phenomenon. Every society is held together by a shared, public morality. Acts which are performed in private are still the proper concern of the public morality.

> What makes a society of any sort is community of ideas, not only political ideas but also ideas about the way its members should behave and govern their lives; these latter ideas are its morals. . . . Take, for example, the institution of marriage. Whether a man should be allowed to take more than one wife is something about which every society has to make up its own mind one way or the other. . . . Marriage is part of the structure of our society and it is also the basis of a moral code which condemns fornication and adultery. The institution of marriage would be gravely threatened if individual judgements were permitted about the morality of adultery; on these matters there must be a public morality. . . . without shared ideas on politics, morals, and ethics no society can exist. . . . For society is not something that is kept together physically; it is held by the invisible bonds of common thought. (pp. 9–10)

Society, therefore, according to Devlin, quite properly concerns itself with infringements of this publicly shared morality. They are threats to society itself, which can no more be indifferent to them than it can to treason. Take the case with which the Wolfenden Report concerned itself—the question whether homosexual behaviour should or should not be illegal. Homosexual acts may not harm others, but in a society built upon the institution of heterosexual marriage they are, Devlin maintains, a threat to the social order and to the moral code which holds it together. Though they may be 'private' acts in one sense, they are also violations of this public morality. Consequently Devlin cannot accept the reason given for making homosexual behaviour no longer a criminal offence—the claim that there is 'a realm of private morality and immorality which is . . . not the law's business'. For Devlin there is no such realm. That is not to say that the law should punish all infringements of morality. In various ways the price that would have to be paid may be too high; it may, for example, be quite simply impractical, or it may involve too great an interference in people's lives. 'Privacy' in the everyday sense is something which people rightly value, and the intrusion of law-enforcement agencies into one's own home or into the intimate activities of one's personal life would be held to be unacceptable. Thus, though the condemnation of adultery may be part of society's moral code, the legal prohibition of adultery is not something that could be upheld except by methods which most people would find intolerable. Devlin could in principle allow that the legal prohibition of homosexuality would be undesirable for the same reason. This would not, however, be because it lies on one side of a clear line between private morality and public morality, for according to Devlin there is no such line.

Devlin represents, then, a tradition of thought which rejects the fundamental terms of Mill's enquiry. Mill, we saw, assumes that freedom is to be secured primarily by allotting to 'society' and to 'the individual' their proper spheres. Individuals are free if society does not interfere in those of their activities which do not harm others. But it is precisely this dichotomy between 'the individual' and 'society' that Mill's opponents would reject. The problem is not just that the line between actions which do and actions which do not harm others is difficult to draw in practice. Their objection is an objection in principle to the 'individual'/ 'society' opposition. In the light of this objection—and bearing in mind also the tension within Mill's own account between the negative emphasis on freedom as non-interference and the positive emphasis on freedom as self-determination—I turn now to a radically different account of the nature of freedom.

Twenty-one years after the publication of Mill's essay *On Liberty* there appeared another essay on the subject which similarly combined a philosophical perspective with a practical concern for social and political issues. This was a *Lecture on Liberal Legislation and Freedom of Contract* given by T. H.

Green.[10] Unlike Mill, Green was an academic philosopher, who held a teaching post at Oxford until his death in 1882. He was another of the Oxford Hegelians, but of a very different political persuasion from Bradley. He was an active member of the Liberal Party and an important influence on liberal thought in the wider sense, and his 1880 lecture was addressed to a political rather than a philosophical audience. In it he tries to rethink the fundamental principles and ideas of liberalism, to revise its philosophical foundations and to reformulate it in a way which allows a much more positive role for state action. The impact of this new version of liberalism is to be found in the policies adopted by the Liberal Party in the early years of this century.

Green begins from a consideration of various pieces of legislation which had generally been supported by Liberals, but which appeared to increase the authority of the state over the lives of individuals. Two main examples were the series of Factory Acts which regulated the hours of work and the working conditions in factories and mines, and the 1870 Education Act which introduced the principle of compulsory education. 'Here, then', says Green, 'is a great system of restriction, which yet hardly any impartial person wishes to see reversed; which many of us wish to see made more complete' (p. 370). His question is then whether those who advocate such legislation are betraying the cause of individual liberty.

The same examples are, as it happens, discussed by Mill, not in the essay *On Liberty* but in the final chapter of his *Principles of Political Economy*.[11] It will, I think, be illuminating to approach Green's discussion by way of a comparison with Mill. Predictably, Mill is extremely cautious about state intervention, and his emphasis on the dangers draws from him a particularly strong formulation of the idea of freedom as non-interference. 'There is,' he says,

[10] References are to T. H. Green, *Works*, ed. R. L. Nettleship (London 1889). The lecture has recently been reprinted in T. H. Green, *Lectures on the Principles of Political Obligation and Other Writings*, ed. Paul Harris and John Morrow (Cambridge 1986).

[11] References are to J. S. Mill, *Principles of Political Economy*, ed. Donald Winch (Harmondsworth 1970).

a circle around every individual human being, which no government, be it that of one, of a few, or of the many, ought to be permitted to overstep. . . . That there is, or ought to be, some space in human existence thus entrenched around, and sacred from authoritative intrusion, no one who professes the smallest regard to human freedom and dignity will call in question. . . . (p. 306)

This general statement is followed by a consideration of possible exceptions to the principle of government non-interference, in the course of which Mill considers the examples of education and of the Factory Acts. He allows that the case of education may be a legitimate exception. Normally a strong reason against government interference is that the individual is the best judge of his or her own interests; in the case of education, however, this assumption will no longer hold good. 'The uncultivated cannot be competent judges of cultivation.' Only as a result of the process of education itself can children come to recognize that it is in their interests to be educated. Until then, they are not the best judges of their own interests in this respect, and may properly be compelled to learn for their own good. Mill takes the same view in *On Liberty*, where he says that his defence of freedom

is meant to apply only to human beings in the maturity of their faculties. We are not speaking of children, or of young persons below the age which the law may fix as that of manhood or womanhood. Those who are still in a state to require being taken care of by others, must be protected against their own actions as well as against external injury. (p. 135)

Mill therefore allows that it is right for the state to compel all children to be educated up to a certain level—and this is, of course, a compulsion imposed both on parents and on children.[12] Moreover, the government must itself do some-

---

[12] This further complicates the issue, which accordingly concerns not just permissible restrictions on the liberty of children, but also permissible restrictions on the liberty of parents to do what they wish with their children. The latter aspect is, Mill thinks, one of the relatively few cases where the society of his own day errs in the direction of excessive liberty. A parent's treatment of his or her child is clearly a case of action which affects the interests of another, and yet 'one would almost think that a man's children were supposed to be literally, and not metaphorically, a part of himself, so jealous is opinion of the smallest interference of law with his absolute and exclusive control over them' (*On Liberty*, p. 238).

thing to provide this education. On this point there seems to be a difference in emphasis between *Political Economy* and *On Liberty*. In the latter he is opposed to state education.

The objections which are urged with reason against State education do not apply to the enforcement of education by the State, but to the State's taking upon itself to direct that education; which is a totally different thing. That the whole or any large part of the education of the people should be in State hands, I go as far as anyone in deprecating. . . . A general State education is a mere contrivance for moulding people to be exactly like one another. (p. 239)

Mill's general position, then, is that the State should enforce universal education but not provide it. He concedes, however, that 'when society in general is in so backward a state that it could not or would not provide for itself any proper institutions of education unless the government undertook the task: then, indeed, the government may, as the less of two great evils, take upon itself the business of schools and universities' (p. 240). In *Political Economy* he seems to take the view that the England of his own day is in just such a backward condition, and that therefore the government cannot consistently require universal education without also undertaking to provide it.

It is therefore an allowable exercise of the powers of government, to impose on parents the legal obligation of giving elementary instruction to children. This however cannot fairly be done, without taking measures to ensure that such instruction shall be always accessible to them, either gratuitously or at a trifling expense. (p. 319)

The efforts of the voluntary School Societies to provide education are regarded by Mill as totally inadequate in quantity and quality. 'I hold it therefore the duty of the government to supply the defect by giving pecuniary support to elementary schools, such as to render them accessible to all the children of the poor, either freely, or for a payment too inconsiderable to be sensibly felt.' (pp. 320–1)

Even so, Mill remains cautious about advocating state education, and sensitive to what he sees as the dangers. He insists that there must be no government monopoly of education, and no compulsion on parents to send their children to state schools if they prefer to educate them elsewhere. We can recognize here the beginnings of a debate which still continues between those who advocate the abolition of private schools and those who claim that this would be an unwarranted intrusion upon the freedom of parents to decide what kind of education they want for their children.

Here, then, is a case where Mill allows an exception to the presumption against government interference, but is cautious about doing so and acutely conscious of the dangers. The same can be said of his attitude to the Factory Acts. The growth of this body of legislation had been achieved by a combination of working class agitation and the campaigning of Tory philanthropists. It had been strenuously opposed by many of the employers, who invoked the slogan 'freedom of contract'. Employers and employees, they argued, should be free to make contracts with one another on whatever terms they chose; if these terms committed the workers to work for long hours or in dangerous conditions, that was simply a matter between them and their employers, and not one with which the government had any right to concern itself. The legislation was, in fact, successful only because it came to be accepted that the principle of 'freedom of contract' did not apply to women and children, who were not really capable of making contracts on their own behalf. Consequently the Acts limited hours of work only for women and children, though their practical effect was to set the same limits for men too.

Mill accepts the case for legislation as it applies to children. His reasons are the same as they were in the matter of education. Children are not fully competent judges of their own interests. They are not in a position to make genuinely free contracts, and therefore legal safeguards are needed to ensure that labour contracts do not exploit them. Mill is adamant, however, that this argument does not apply to women. He is firmly committed to the principle of sexual equality and to the cause of the emancipation of women, and will therefore have no truck with any suggestion that women's employment contracts have to be made for them by men. 'Women', he says, 'are as capable as men of appreciating and managing their own concerns, and the only hindrance to their doing so arises from the injustice of their present social position' (p. 324). Since a principal means of escape from 'their present social position' lies in their opportunities for independent employment, Mill is opposed to any legal restriction of such opportunities.

With children the case is different. 'Freedom of contract, in the case of children, is but another word for freedom of coercion' (p. 323). Mill therefore accepts the need for legislation dealing with child labour and assumes a clear-cut division between adults, to whom the idea of 'freedom of contract' is applicable, and children, to whom it is not. But is the division really so clear-cut? Let us remind ourselves of the conditions in which the mid-nineteenth-century factory worker might have to accept employment. Suppose that he has to choose between working for long hours and for low wages in atrocious conditions, or starving because he has no work at all. If he chooses to work on those terms, can he really be said to have made a 'free contract'?

It is this question of the relation between 'liberal legislation' and 'freedom of contract' which prompts the title of T. H. Green's lecture. Let us now turn to his treatment of the same examples. We find that where Mill cautiously allows exceptions to the principle of government non-interference, Green is an enthusiastic advocate of the Factory Acts and of the 1870 Education Act. He sees them not merely as legitimate exceptions, but as positive enhancements of people's freedom. To make good this interpretation of them, he needs to offer an alternative account of the concept of freedom, and this he does in a crucial paragraph which, long as it is, should be quoted in full.

We shall probably all agree that freedom, rightly understood, is the greatest of blessings; that its attainment is the true end of all our effort as citizens. But when we thus speak of freedom, we should consider carefully what we mean by it. We do not mean merely freedom from restraint or compulsion. We do not mean merely freedom to do as we like irrespectively of what it is that we like. We do not mean a freedom that can be enjoyed by one man or one set of men at the cost of a loss of freedom to others. When we speak of freedom as something to be so highly prized, we mean a positive power or capacity of doing or enjoying something worth doing or enjoying, and that, too, something that we do or enjoy in common with others. We mean by it a power which each man exercises through the help or security given him by his fellow-men, and which he in turn helps to secure for them. When we measure the progress of a society by its growth in freedom, we measure it by the increasing development and exercise on the whole of those powers of contributing to social good with which we believe the members of the society to be endowed; in short, by the greater power on the part of the citizens as a body to make the most and best of themselves. Thus, though of course there can be no freedom among men who act not willingly but under compulsion, yet on the other hand the mere removal of compulsion, the mere enabling a man to do as he likes, is in itself no contribution to true freedom. In one sense no man is so well able to do as he likes as the wandering savage. He has no master. There is no one to say him nay. Yet we do not count him really free, because the freedom of savagery is not strength, but weakness. The actual powers of the noblest savage do not admit of comparison with those of the humblest citizen of a law-abiding state. He is not the slave of man, but he is the slave of nature. Of compulsion by natural necessity he has plenty of experience, though of restraint by society none at all. Nor can he deliver himself from that compulsion except by submitting to this restraint. So to submit is the first step in true freedom, because the first step towards the full exercise of the faculties with which man is endowed. But we rightly refuse to recognise the highest development on the part of an exceptional individual or exceptional class, as an advance towards the true freedom of man, if it is founded on a refusal of the same opportunity to other men. The powers of the human mind have probably never attained such force and keenness, the proof of what society can do for the individual has never been so strikingly exhibited, as among the small groups of men who possessed civil privileges in the small republics of antiquity. The whole framework of our political ideas, to say nothing of our philosophy, is derived from them. But in them this extraordinary efflorescence of the privileged class was accompanied by the slavery of the multitude. That slavery was the condition on which it depended, and for that reason it was doomed to decay. There is no clearer ordinance of that supreme reason, often dark to us, which governs the course of man's affairs, than that no body of men should in the long run be able to strengthen itself at the cost of others' weakness. The civilisation and freedom of the ancient world were shortlived because they were partial and exceptional. If the

ideal of true freedom is the maximum of power for all members of
human society alike to make the best of themselves, we are right in
refusing to ascribe the glory of freedom to a state in which the
apparent elevation of the few is founded on the degradation of the
many, and in ranking modern society, founded as it is on free
industry, with all its confusion and ignorant licence and waste of
effort, above the most splendid of ancient republics. (pp. 370–2)

This paragraph runs together a number of claims which we
must now disentangle.

Clearly Green does not believe that freedom can be
equated with the mere absence of interference. Though he
thinks that non-interference is a necessary condition of
freedom—'. . . there can be no freedom among men who act
not willingly but under compulsion . . .'—he does not take it
to be a sufficient condition. 'Freedom' in its full sense is not
the negative concept of absence of restraint or absence of
compulsion, but a positive concept.

The core of Green's positive concept of freedom seems to
be the following claim:

(1) Freedom is the development and exercise of one's powers
and capacities.

In distinguishing positive freedom from the mere absence of
compulsion, Green wishes to distinguish it also from merely
doing as one likes, and this leads him to the further claim:

(2) Freedom is a positive power or capacity of doing or
enjoying something worth doing or enjoying.

Green also suggests that freedom in the positive sense defined
by (1) and (2) can exist only in a social context. The isolated
individual cannot develop his powers and capacities; he is
Green's 'wandering savage', a 'slave of nature'. One can
develop one's human capacities only by drawing on the
resources of society. For Green, then, freedom is not only a
positive but also a social phenomenon, and this aspect of the
concept is formulated in three further claims, of increasing
strength. There is first the general claim:

(3) One can be free only in society.

This must be distinguished from the stronger claim:

(4) Freedom is the development and exercise of one's powers
of contributing to social good.

One might, by living in society, develop one's powers and capacities and yet use them to promote one's own individual good rather than the good of one's society. In respect of claim (3) this would count as true freedom, but not in respect of claim (4). Different again is the further claim:

(5) The development of the powers and capacities of some members of a society is not an advance towards the true freedom of man if it is denied to other members of that society.

This seems to amount to saying that freedom is not true freedom unless it is shared by everyone. It is thus distinct from claims (3) and (4). In the city-states of antiquity to which Green refers, the citizens may well have developed their powers and capacities by participating in the life of their community, and they may have used those powers and capacities to contribute to the good of their community, but those same advantages were not shared by the slaves. Consequently they cannot, according to Green, count as 'an advance towards true freedom'.

I shall turn in a moment to the assessment of the various claims, but first let us consider how they shape Green's view of the examples of 'liberal legislation'. Of the Factory Acts he says:

Every injury to the health of the individual is, so far as it goes, a public injury. It is an impediment to the general freedom; so much deduction from our power, as members of society, to make the best of ourselves. Society is, therefore, plainly within its right when it limits freedom of contract for the sale of labour, so far as is done by our laws for the sanitary regulations of factories, workshops, and mines. It is equally within its right in prohibiting the labour of women and young persons beyond certain hours. (p. 373)

Notice the implicit contradiction of Mill; an injury to the individual is at the same time, inescapably, a public injury, and therefore not just a matter for the individual. More fundamental to Green's argument, however, is the appeal to the notion of freedom as self-development; degrading and debilitating work prevents people from developing their faculties, as such it is an impediment to their freedom, and hence laws which prohibit such work help to promote people's freedom. The same reasoning is at work in Green's comments on the Education Act:

Without a command of certain elementary arts and knowledge, the individual in modern society is as effectually crippled as by the loss of a limb or a broken constitution. He is not free to develop his faculties. With a view to securing such freedom among its members it is . . . within the province of the state to prevent children growing up in that kind of ignorance which practically excludes them from a free career in life. . . . (p. 373–4)

In short, compulsory education enables people to develop their faculties and thus promotes their freedom.

Green goes on to consider other examples, such as legislation restricting the sale of land, and 'temperance' legislation limiting the sale of alcoholic drink. But the lecture is not just concerned with isolated examples. The Factory Acts and the Education Act are instances of a general tendency of legislation in the modern state aimed at securing by collective means the welfare of its citizens. We can see in them the beginnings of the modern welfare state, and the question which concerns Green is, in effect, whether we should see in the welfare state a friend or a foe to liberty. At one level it is undeniably coercive. Such legislation compels all members of society to contribute, through the payment of taxes, to the collective provision of welfare. Nevertheless, Green would claim that by providing people with education and good health and decent living conditions, it helps to promote their freedom. Clearly our view of the welfare state must be affected by whether we can accept Green's claim.

We have seen that his defence of it appeals to a positive and social concept of freedom. That too is not an isolated suggestion. Like the reinterpretation of the individual–society relation which we considered earlier, it derives from Hegel and is characteristic of the Hegelian philosophical tradition. It is also a further example of the influence of Hegel on Marxist thought. In Marx's and Engels's early work *The German Ideology* we find the following, thoroughly Hegelian, statement: 'Only in community [with others has each] individual the means of cultivating his gifts in all directions;

only in the community, therefore, is personal freedom possible.'[13]

Marx and Engels never devoted much attention to the details of this view of freedom, but Engels in his later writings sometimes returned to it. Like Green he maintains that freedom is possible only in society, because only through the historical growth of human society do we acquire the scientific understanding and the technological means which enable us to master and control nature. 'Freedom therefore consists in the control over ourselves and over external nature, a control founded on knowledge of natural necessity; it is therefore necessarily a product of historical development.'[14]

Notice, however, that Engels adds a new emphasis. Freedom involves control not just over natural forces but also 'over ourselves'—that is, over social forces. In a class-divided society, and especially in a market economy, these social forces acquire an independence and a momentum of their own; since we act not collectively but individually and competitively, the consequences of our innumerable individual actions escape human control and become blind forces dominating us like natural forces. Only in a classless society, in which the means of production are communally owned and collectively managed, can these forces be brought under free conscious human control.

Man's own social organisation, hitherto confronting him as a necessity imposed by nature and history, now becomes the result of his own free action. The extraneous objective forces that have hitherto governed history pass under the control of man himself. Only from that time will man himself, with full consciousness, make his own history—only from that time will the social causes set in movement by him have, in the main and in a constantly growing measure, the results intended by him. It is the ascent of man from the kingdom of necessity to the kingdom of freedom. (ibid., p. 336)

The positive and social concept of freedom, then, is espoused not just by individual philosophers but by a continuing philosophical tradition. The two broad ways of

[13] K. Marx and F. Engels, *The German Ideology, Part One*, ed. C. J. Arthur (London 1970), p. 83.
[14] F. Engels, *Anti-Dühring: Herr Eugen Dühring's Revolution in Science* (Moscow and London 1969), p. 137.

thinking about freedom—as a negative and as a positive concept—have been contrasted by a modern philosopher, Isaiah Berlin, in a lecture entitled 'Two Concepts of Liberty' (1958).[15] Berlin is primarily concerned not with particular philosophers but with the general directions taken by these two conflicting lines of thought. Although he does not set out to argue for or against either of them, it becomes clear that he sees the tendency of the 'positive' tradition as especially dangerous. The positive concept is, he says, one 'which the adherents of the "negative" notion represent as being, at times, no better than a specious disguise for brutal tyranny' (p. 131).

Looking back at some of Green's claims we can see why this might be so. Recall Green's claim (2): 'Freedom is a positive power or capacity of doing or enjoying something worth doing or enjoying.' This seems to suggest that if I am doing or enjoying something which is not really worth doing or enjoying, I am not genuinely free. But who is to say what is worth doing or enjoying? In the absence of a satisfactory answer to that question, the way seems to be open for any tyrant to coerce people into doing what he thinks is worth doing, and to say that he is, in Rousseau's ominous words, simply 'forcing them to be free'.[16] Even more open to abuse is Green's claim (4): 'Freedom is the development and exercise of one's powers of contributing to social good.' One would normally suppose that it is possible for people to be acting freely, yet freely choose not to contribute to social good. Green, however, is apparently committed to saying that if I am not contributing to social good, I cannot really be acting freely; consequently, if I am forcibly prevented from pursuing my own anti-social objectives, I am not being deprived of anything which genuinely deserves to be called 'freedom'. As Berlin comments, 'Green was a genuine liberal: but many a tyrant could use this formula to justify his worst acts of oppression' (p. 133 n.).

These, then, are the dangers which Berlin sees lurking in the positive concept. Nor are they simply the dangers of philosophical confusion. 'Recent history has made it only too

---

[15] References are to Isaiah Berlin, *Four Essays on Liberty*, (Oxford 1969).
[16] Jean-Jacques Rousseau, *The Social Contract* (1762), Book I, ch. 7.

clear', according to Berlin, 'that the issue is not merely academic' (p. 134). He has in mind the so-called 'totalitarian' regimes of the twentieth century, and the intellectual sleight of hand which has been used to justify them. Berlin does not supply examples (the paucity of examples is an annoying feature of his lecture), but we can do so. Consider an essay by Christopher Caudwell entitled 'Liberty—a Study in Bourgeois Illusion', published in 1938.[17] For the most part this is an admirably clear exposition of the Marxist view that the growth of freedom consists in the development of men's collective powers to control both the natural environment and their own social world. But now consider this passage:

Any definition of liberty is humbug that does not mean this: liberty to do what one wants. A people is free whose members have liberty to do what they want—to get the goods they desire and avoid the ills they hate. What do men want? They want to be happy, and not be starved or despised or deprived of the decencies of life. They want to be secure, and friendly with their fellows, and not conscripted to slaughter and be slaughtered. They want to marry, and beget children, and help, not oppress each other. Who is free who cannot do these things, even if he has a vote, and free speech? Who then is free in bourgeois society, for not a few men but millions are forced by circumstances to be unemployed, and miserable, and despised, and unable to enjoy the decencies of life? (p. 225)

This account prepares the ground for Caudwell then to claim that

as Russia shows, even in the dictatorship of the proletariat, before the classless State has come into being, man is already freer. He can avoid unemployment, and competition with his fellows, and poverty. He can marry and beget children, and achieve the decencies of life. He is not asked to oppress his fellows. (p. 227)

The régime which Caudwell is trying to justify here is the Stalinist regime of the thirties, with its purges, show trials, forced labour and forced collectivization of agriculture. Whatever we may count as the achievements of that régime,

[17] References are to Christopher Caudwell, *Studies in a Dying Culture* (London 1938). The essay is reprinted in Christopher Caudwell, *The Concept of Freedom* (London 1965).

the promotion of freedom is hardly likely to figure prominently in the list, and if the positive concept of freedom leads to a view of Stalinism as an advance in freedom, we may reasonably have our doubts about the concept.

Stalinism was undoubtedly one of the examples that Berlin had in mind. The other was Fascism, and Berlin would, I think, be one of those political philosophers who would link Stalinist Russia with Hitler's Germany and Mussolini's Italy under the general heading of 'totalitarianism'. Here is a passage from an essay by Alfredo Rocco, one of Mussolini's ministers and advisers:

There is a Liberal theory of freedom, and there is a Fascist concept of liberty. For we, too, maintain the necessity of safeguarding the conditions that make for the free development of the individual; we, too, believe that the oppression of individual personality can find no place in the modern state. We do not, however, accept a bill of rights which tends to make the individual superior to the state and to empower him to act in opposition to society. Our concept of liberty is that the individual must be allowed to develop his personality on behalf of the state. . . . Freedom therefore is due to the citizen and to classes on condition that they exercise it in the interest of society as a whole and within the limits set by social exigencies, liberty being, like any other individual right, a concession of the state.[18]

Rocco's 'concept of liberty'—'that the individual must be allowed to develop his personality in behalf of the state'—is directly reminiscent of Green. If it can be used to legitimate Fascism, what does this tell us about Green's account?

To answer that question we must now undertake a direct assessment of Green's positive concept of liberty, as contained in the five claims which I identified.

---

[18] Alfredo Rocco, 'The Political Doctrine of Fascism', reprinted in *Readings on Fascism and National Socialism* selected by members of the Department of Philosophy, University of Colorado (Chicago 1952), pp. 35–6.

# 3

## The Nature of Freedom

THE first of the claims which I attributed to Green was:

(1) Freedom is the development and exercise of one's powers and capacities.

At this point there is common ground between Green and Mill. Though I have contrasted Green's positive concept with Mill's stress on the negative idea of non-interference, we saw that there is a positive strand in Mill's account also. I located it in his appeal to the ideal of the 'fully human life'—the ideal of living one's life to the full by making use of one's distinctively human capacities. Mill thinks that 'the human faculties of perception, judgment, discriminative feeling, mental activity, and even moral preference, are exercised only in making a choice' (*On Liberty*, p. 187). I want to suggest that it is this notion of 'making a choice' that we should hang on to, as providing the firm and clear link with the concept of freedom. Intuitively, the idea of choice seems to me to be the core of our idea of freedom. I shall now try to give strength to this intuitive impression, by trying to show that if we anchor our account of freedom in the notion of choice, we can then see clearly how other aspects of freedom fit into the picture, and why they *are* aspects of freedom. Already, indeed, we have made a start on this task, for I have suggested that we can understand the link between freedom and the development of one's faculties when we see how they are connected via the notion of making a choice.

It is along these same lines, then, that we can understand the relation between freedom and the negative idea of 'non-interference'. If you are free in so far as you are in a position to make choices, then you will lack freedom to the extent that other people prevent you making choices, or make them for you. This is not to say that freedom can simply be identified with 'being left alone', or 'not being interfered with', or even 'not being restricted or coerced'. But if we identify freedom with being able to make choices, then we can see that the absence of coercion is one of the important *conditions* which help to put one in a position to make choices. This is something which Green would not deny; he allows that 'of course there can be no freedom among men who act not willingly but under compulsion . . .' The sentence continues: 'yet on the other hand the mere removal of compulsion, the mere enabling a man to do as he likes, is in itself no contribution to true freedom'. That is too strong, I think. The removal of compulsion is some contribution to freedom. But it is not the whole of freedom. It is merely one condition among others.

Why should we put the emphasis this way round? Why say that the notion of 'making choices' is primary, and that the absence of coercion is relevant to freedom only as a condition for the making of choices? Why not say, for example, that 'being able to make choices' and 'not being coerced' are equal components in the definition of freedom, two sides of the same coin? The answer is, I think, that only when the idea of making choices is already presupposed can certain kinds of circumstances count as the absence of coercion. The merely negative fact of being left alone does not, simply in itself, count as the removal of coercion. A rock or a stone does not become free by being left alone and not interfered with. Talk of coercion and its absence only makes sense when applied to the kind of being which could make choices. And even in the case of human beings the removal of certain physical states of affairs counts as the removal of coercion only if there are choices which that person wants to make and which are affected by the presence or absence of those states of affairs.

But still, it may be said, though talk of 'freedom' and 'coercion' applies only to beings who could make choices, the fact remains that it is the absence of coercion that *constitutes* their freedom. In reply I think we should emphasize, as Green does, that our account of freedom must explain what makes freedom a value. What we take to be central to the concept of freedom should be whatever it is that makes freedom important to us. Now in so far as we value freedom, what we value is not the mere negative fact of being left alone. In many contexts that may be something that has no value at all; or we may want to be left alone for quite other reasons—because we are feeling depressed, perhaps, or uncommunicative. When it is connected with our valuing of freedom, we wish not to be interfered with by others precisely because, and only because, that will enable us to make our own choices for ourselves.

Green says: 'When we speak of freedom as something to be so highly prized, we mean a positive power or capacity of doing or enjoying something worth doing or enjoying . . .' He is wrong to infer that freedom is valuable only in so far as it enables us to do something valuable. Whatever it is that we do, the very fact that in doing it we exercise our freedom is to that extent something valuable and important. But it is valuable because it is the exercise of our capacity to make choices for ourselves, and that is why we should put the making of choices at the centre of our concept of freedom.

So far, then, I have suggested that the central element in the concept of freedom is the positive one of being able to make choices, and that the negative fact of non-interference is related to it as one of the conditions for our being able to make choices. Certainly the connection between non-interference and freedom is a close one. It is not that the former just happens sometimes to promote the latter. Rather, the coercive or restrictive interference by some people in the actions of others is one of the characteristic ways in which freedom is negated. But still, freedom is not straightforwardly identical with the absence of interference or coercion.

Now if there are characteristic negative conditions of freedom, there are also certain characteristic positive conditions. To see this, we should notice first that freedom is not a mere matter of being able to make just any choice at all. It depends crucially on the range of choice. There are degrees of freedom, and, other things being equal, the greater the range of choices open to me, the freer I am. Compare a prisoner chained to the walls of his cell, a person under house arrest, someone who lives in a country where there are strict travel restrictions, and someone who lives in a country where he can travel to any part of it or leave it altogether. Each person in the sequence is freer than the one before, because he has more options open to him, more places to which he can go.

The range of choice is not just a matter of the sheer number of options. One's degree of freedom depends not only on the quantitative range but also on the qualitative range of choice. My freedom is not increased by the availability of a large number of options if there is, as we say, 'nothing to choose between them'. A notorious example is the availability of innumerable brands of some commodity. If the local shop stocks ten different brands of pork pie, indistinguishable except for the wrapping, my freedom of choice is not thereby increased. On the other hand, if it were to stock different kinds of pie, with different kinds of filling, some of them home-made and some of them mass-produced, this does genuinely increase my freedom of choice—not greatly, for the choice of foods is not one of the most important choices I have to make, but significantly none the less. And the more important the options are that are open to me, the greater the difference they make to my freedom. If my freedom is increased by the choice of foods available to me, it is increased more significantly by the choice of political parties for which I can vote—unless of course, as sometimes happens, the parties are as indistinguishable as pork pies. Again, more important than the choice of foods will be the choice of religious or moral or philosophical beliefs which I can espouse, for these are likely to be more fundamental to my life and to my sense of my own identity. So in maintaining that freedom consists in being able to make choices, we must add that the degree of freedom is determined not by the sheer number of choices available, but by the range of meaningful choice. And here the phrase 'range of meaningful choice' must refer both to the areas of people's lives in which they can make choices and the options from which they can choose.

Emphasizing the notion of 'meaningful' choice makes it possible to deal with an objection which has been formulated in terms of the following counter-example:

The range of physical possibilities from which a person can choose at a given moment has no direct relevance to freedom. The rock climber on a difficult pitch who sees only one way out to save his life is unquestionably free, though we would hardly say he has any choice . . . Whether [a person] is free or not does not depend on the range of choice.[1]

Now of course if the rock-climber's only concern is to save his life, it does not matter to him whether he has any choice of ways in which to do it—indeed, in that context the question of his freedom does not even arise. In other contexts, however, the availability of various difficult routes might well matter to him. From the point of view of his desire to exercise his skills as a rock climber, he would want to be able to do different kinds of climb which posed different kinds of challenge for him. Suppose that the range of climbs he could do were drastically curtailed—suppose, perhaps, that whole areas of the mountains were taken over by the military for training purposes. Since this represents a curtailment of options which are important for him, it can now be properly described as a diminution of his freedom of choice.

Consider now another objection. It may be said that this emphasis on the range of choice is a distortedly 'consumerist' view of freedom. It seems to suggest that we need to be presented with a varied array of commodities from which we can be constantly choosing. But, the objection may run, many people don't want this endless variety, they have a fixed and settled way of life to which they are committed, and freedom to them means simply being left to get on with living their own life in their own way. However, if this is to count as the exercise of freedom, it must be the case that the way of life to which they are committed is one which they have genuinely chosen. They may not want to go on making an endless succession of choices, but it is still important that they should have made their own choice in the first place. It must therefore have been the case that a significant range of alternatives was open to them, for their choice to be a real one. Moreover, for a society to be one in which different people can make their varying choices of activities and ways of life, the range of choices open to them must reflect the range of differing human interests and temperaments.

This may now seem to raise a further difficulty. If people differ in their interests, so that what is important to one may

[1] F. A. Hayek, *The Constitution of Liberty* (London 1960), pp. 12–13.

be quite unimportant to another, can we give any definite and objective meaning to the phrase 'range of meaningful choice'? Will it not follow that what counts as a meaningful choice for one person will, for another, be no significant choice at all? What, for the gourmet, is a range of subtly different tastes may for the rest of us, with our more insensitive palates, be simply a choice of indistinguishables. Our rock climber may want a choice of pitches which provide him with a diversity of challenges, but for the rest of us they are just a bunch of rocks. Does not the notion of 'meaningful choice' then become hopelessly subjective?

Not hopelessly so. For a start, though people vary, they vary in ways which are themselves fairly constant. At least within the limits of a broad historical epoch, there is a certain predictability to the range of human interests and concerns, and the claims of any society to be a free society will in part depend on how adequately that range is reflected in the kinds of activities open to people in that society. For some people religious beliefs will matter not at all, but for others they will certainly matter a great deal, and a society which eliminated all opportunities for religious practices and observances on the grounds that these were of no importance could not plausibly claim to be a particularly free society. For some people, again, cultural activities will be of fundamental importance, and for others, opportunities for physical exercise and recreation, and any society in which such opportunities are not available or are drastically curtailed will be to that extent less free—even though not everyone will want to be able to make such choices.

Moreover, there is sufficient constancy in human beings for us to be able to say at least something about what would or would not count as a meaningful choice for *anyone*. Notice that if this were not so, we could give no account of the notion of 'coercion'. Coercion does not consist in the total physical control of one person by another. The closest one could come to that would be, I suppose, for a prisoner to be so securely shackled to the wall of his cell that he could move none of his limbs. That, however, is not a typical case of coercion. Typically, someone who is coerced does, in one sense, have a choice—but it is a case of coercion precisely because the choice is not a meaningful choice. The victim of an armed robbery is given a choice—'Your money or your life.' But the choice is not such as to make him free, for the option of parting with one's life is not normally a real option. There are exceptions even here, and the would-be suicide's response to the threat may be 'Take my life, it's useless to me.' Normally, however, the continuation of one's life is as important to a person as anything can be, and that is why 'Your money or your life' is a coercive threat, not a meaningful choice.

I submit, then, that how free one is will depend not just on one's being able to make choices at all, but on one's scope for choice—on the range of meaningful choices open to one. This range will be both objectively and subjectively determined. It will be a matter both of what options are as a matter of fact available, and of one's subjective ability to envisage and assess alternatives. Consequently, the characteristic conditions of freedom include not only the negative condition of not being coerced or restricted, but also certain positive conditions. These fall into the main categories of political conditions, material conditions, and cultural conditions. I shall look at each of these in turn.

## POLITICAL CONDITIONS

It seems plausible to suppose that institutional arrangements which give me some degree of political power will, to that extent, increase my capacity to make choices about the affairs of the society in which I live, and therefore also about my own life. In other words, an increase in democracy would seem to be an increase in freedom. That has indeed been a common assumption both of political philosophers and of political movements, but it has not gone unchallenged. Mill, we saw, warns against the 'the tyranny of the majority'. Political self-government, he says, 'is not the government of each by himself, but of each by all the rest' (*On Liberty*, p. 129), and in practice that means the government of each individual by the majority of the people. Berlin takes up the theme:

Just as a democracy may, in fact, deprive the individual citizen of a great many liberties which he might have in some other form of society, so it is perfectly conceivable that a liberal-minded despot would allow his subjects a large measure of personal freedom. . . . Freedom in this sense is not, at any rate logically, connected with democracy or self-government. Self-government may, on the whole, provide a better guarantee of the preservation of civil liberties than other regimes, and has been defended as such by libertarians. But there is no necessary connection between individual liberty and democratic rule. The answer to the question 'Who governs me?' is logically distinct from the question 'How far does government interfere with me?' It is in this difference that the great contrast between the two concepts of negative and positive liberty, in the end, consists. (pp. 129–30)

I am concerned to deny that there is a 'great contrast' here. The negative and the positive aspects of liberty have equally to do with the single question 'How much scope do I have to make choices about my own life?', and that scope may be limited both by the interference of those who hold political power, and by my own lack of political power.

The difficulty is, of course, that though democratic political arrangements may give me the power to make choices, that power has to be exercised collectively. I must share it with others. However, the fact that choices are made collectively does not by itself mean that they cease to be real choices. Consider first a small-scale example. Suppose that I am on a walking holiday with a couple of friends. Each day we have to decide where we shall walk. This may involve a good deal of discussion, the weighing of suggestions and counter-suggestions, and a willingness on the part of each of us to make compromises. If we decide in that way, we may quite properly be said to have chosen collectively, and thereby to have exercised our collective freedom. By comparison with a group which has to follow a route laid down for them, we are perfectly free to decide where to go, albeit we must decide jointly. Now of course things may not turn out that way. At the other extreme, it may be that the other two have some kind of hold over me—perhaps they have all the money, so that I have to go where they go—and they take no account of my wishes; we always decide 'democratically', but

I am always outvoted by two to one. If we turn our attention now from the small-scale example to larger-scale political institutions, this becomes increasingly a possibility—that my views are of no account and I am constantly out-voted. What does this show? Certainly in such cases I have no real choice about what happens. This does not, however, sever the link between freedom and political power, for it also has to be said that in such cases I have no real political power. If democracy means the sharing of political power, it requires more than just that everyone should have a vote, for if one is in a permanent minority that vote confers no effective power. The ideal of democracy would be that everyone is listened to, that everyone's views are taken account of and that proposals are formulated and reformulated in the light of discussion and argument. To the extent that this ideal is realized, people have political power, they participate in the collective making of choices, and their freedom is increased.

I have referred to it as the ideal of democracy, but the response may be that this ideal is utterly remote from reality. I have no doubt that this response is too simple, and that in very small groups or institutions democratic decision-making can take something like that form. The question is whether anything approaching it is at all possible in large institutions such as the modern nation-state. There are huge problems here, and I shall return to them in later chapters. For the moment I simply want to maintain the connection between political power and freedom, and to suggest that that connection cannot be disproved by a cursory reference to modern democratic institutions. We should not be misled by the fact that these institutions do not seem greatly to increase our freedom. Rather, that should prompt us to ask how democratic they really are. My claim, at any rate, is that in so far as these institutions give us any political power at all, to that extent they increase our freedom.

## MATERIAL CONDITIONS

I use the phrase 'material conditions' to refer to a wide range of phenomena. In contemporary society, I suppose, the most obvious example of the liberating character of material conditions is that of monetary wealth. If I inherit a fortune or win the pools or, less spectacularly, get a new job which will provide a larger income, new opportunities become available to me which were previously inaccessible; I can travel to different places, engage in different activities or pastimes—new worlds, geographically new or culturally new, are opened up for me. The connection with freedom lies not in the greater material comforts or enjoyments but in the increase of possibilities—the greater scope for choice.

Material wealth, though it may be the most obvious, is not the only example. I have in mind also the way in which the provision of material goods and the satisfaction of basic material needs may liberate people's energies. Poverty and material deprivation make it difficult for people to lift their sights above the desperate struggle for survival. A greater degree of material affluence changes that; people can then direct their attention elsewhere, can turn their thoughts and their energies to new possibilities.

Under the heading of 'material conditions' I also have in mind the liberating effects of technical progress. In part this is again a matter of the release of energies: when the tedious drudgery of, for example, domestic tasks can be off-loaded onto washing machines and vacuum cleaners, time and energy are made available for other activities and thus people have more choice as to how to spend their lives. Technological developments not only introduce labour-saving ways of performing old tasks; they also introduce entirely new possibilities. They facilitate travel and communication on a much wider scale for many more people; they facilitate the exchange of goods and so extend the range of material commodities which people can enjoy; they bring cultural activities and enjoyments within the reach of many more people. And not only do they make new opportunities available to people generally, they also help to remove some of the particular restrictions previously experienced by specific groups of people. Those who are physically handicapped in some way, for instance—blind, or deaf, or paralysed—can have restored to them, through new medical techniques and other technical resources, many options which would previously have been foreclosed.

Now the relevance of these various material conditions to freedom is, as I have said, that they make available opportunities for choice. I want to insist upon this, because the connection has often been misstated. That, for instance, is the fault with the passage which I quoted from Caudwell. He slides all too easily from defining freedom as doing what you want to defining it as getting what you want, and thence to the claim that if people can avoid poverty and unemployment, and can marry and beget children, they have got what they want and are therefore free. This is a distortion of the concept of freedom, and a distortion which is dangerous for the reasons which Berlin has indicated. A benevolent tyrant may do much for the material prosperity of his subjects, ensuring that they are well-fed and well-clothed and well-housed, but if he also dictates to them how they are to live their lives, he cannot be said to have given them freedom. Material prosperity and freedom are not the same thing, and material goods do not increase people's freedom simply because they are what people want. If they do so, it is because they increase people's opportunities for choice. Normally they do that, but if those opportunities are then cut off in other ways, the freedom will have disappeared even though the prosperity remains.

Some would go further. Berlin, for instance, is sometimes inclined to maintain not just that freedom and material goods are distinct, but that they are altogether unconnected. It may be, he tends to argue, that those who are half-naked and underfed and diseased need clothes and food and medicine more than they need freedom, and may even have to acquire them at the cost of freedom, but if that is so, let us be clear about it and not try to pretend that what they are acquiring is some special sort of freedom—'economic freedom', perhaps.

Why this reluctance to accept the connection between freedom and material goods? Partly, I suppose, because it is sometimes supported by bad arguments of the kind which I have criticized. But I think that another idea is also at work—the idea that the presence or absence of freedom is essentially a matter of direct human intervention, whereas material prosperity or poverty is less clearly a human creation. 'Coercion', according to Berlin, 'implies the deliberate interference of other human beings within the area in which I could otherwise act' (p. 122); consequently 'if I say that I am unable to jump more than ten feet in the air, or cannot read because I am blind, or cannot understand the darker pages of Hegel, it would be eccentric to say that I am to that degree enslaved or coerced'. A reluctance to admit any close connection between material conditions and freedom may therefore stem from the thought that if I am prevented by my poverty from doing various things, no human being is actively restricting me, and so my poverty cannot be described as a limitation on my freedom. But as Berlin himself immediately goes on to recognize, the distinction is not so clear-cut.

If my poverty were a kind of disease, which prevented me from buying bread, or paying for a journey round the world or getting my case heard [in the law courts], as lameness prevents me from running, this inability would not naturally be described as a lack of freedom, least of all political freedom. It is only because I believe that my inability to get a given thing is due to the fact that other human beings have made arrangements whereby I am, whereas others are not, prevented from having enough money with which to pay for it, that I think myself a victim of coercion or slavery. (p. 122–3)

But the fact is that people's relative degree of material prosperity *is* very largely a consequence of humanly created social arrangements. Even the case of lameness, which Berlin offers as an unequivocally natural, non-human check on one's actions, is a case where human social arrangements make a vital difference.Whether my lameness can be cured will depend very largely on whether I can afford to pay for treatment, what kinds of medical facilities are communally provided, and to whom; and thus my opportunities for running will be promoted or restricted by the kind of society I live in and my place within it.

The close connections between material conditions, political power, and freedom are exhibited in the example of 'freedom of contract' which we considered earlier. Suppose that a working man in mid-nineteenth-century Britain is in a situation where he has to choose between working in a factory for long hours in atrocious conditions, or starving. In some sense he has a choice; but we have seen that if one person presents another with a choice between performing a certain action or losing his life, that is a paradigm case of coercion, not freedom. Now in our present example the starkness of the choice is not, perhaps, deliberately imposed on the worker in that way by the factory-owner. The latter may quite genuinely protest that he wishes the situation were different—wishes that more choices were available to the workers, wishes that the pressure of competition did not make it difficult for him to offer better terms of employment, and so on. Nevertheless the stark choice between working and starving, though it is not imposed by any identifiable human agents, is imposed by human social arrangements. The impoverished urban proletariat is a direct product of rural dispossession. The workers' lack of bargaining power is the obverse of the legally-backed absolute power enjoyed by the factory-owner in virtue of his ownership. And this structured distribution of powers and property is one which could have been changed by conscious human agency. Consequently it has to be said that the mid-nineteenth-century worker's lack of powers of choice does represent a lack of freedom, and that to that extent the terms of employment which he accepts cannot be described as a 'free contract'. The example also indicates clearly that 'freedom of contract' is not a matter of 'all or nothing'. The degree of choice available to the worker will be affected by such factors as the general level of prosperity and the availability of work elsewhere; the ability of the workers to combine in trade unions to demand better terms of employment; and the communal provision of benefits to the unemployed which ensure that unemployment is not simply synonymous with starvation. Not that the presence of such factors creates 'freedom of contract' pure and simple—but the more they are present, the greater the degree of freedom.

CULTURAL CONDITIONS

Material conditions are primarily objective determinants of the degree of choice. They determine the range of options which are, objectively, available to a person. But we have noted that one's ability to make choices is also subjectively determined. It depends on the extent to which one is psychologically capable of envisaging alternatives, formulating them clearly and assessing them rationally. This is not an ability which all human beings automatically possess. The new-born child possesses it hardly at all. It can simply respond immediately to a few internal and external stimuli. By contrast the notoriously demanding nature of the tyrannical two-year-old is a consequence of the fact that the child has acquired language and can now formulate, not only to others but also to himself or herself, desires for things which are not immediately present. The child can now make choices in a much fuller sense, because he or she is now able to contemplate alternatives in his or her imagination. This is a vital step in the growth of freedom. How far one advances along this road will depend considerably on the education, formal and informal, which one receives. It will depend on the scope of one's imagination, on the range of one's experience and knowledge, on one's ability to predict the consequences of different courses of action and to compare them with one another. If one has lived all one's life in a small self-enclosed community, one will tend automatically to accept the practices of that community; one will be much more capable of envisaging alternatives, and of choosing between them, if one has direct experience of other ways of doing things, or indirect knowledge of other societies, historical knowledge, the stimulus of imaginative literature, and so on. Again, the extent of one's vocabulary will considerably influence one's ability to articulate clearly to oneself the options between which one can choose. In all these respects, then, one's ability to make choices will be extended or diminished by the quality and quantity of the education one receives.

Not only is one's freedom extended by education, it is also restricted by 'mis-education'—by the inculcation of ideas and attitudes which reconcile one to existing circumstances or channel one's choices in certain specific directions. This will be partly a matter of direct and conscious manipulation, as in the form of political propaganda or commercial advertising, but partly a matter also of the unconscious acceptance of the prejudices and thought-patterns of one's own community. Consequently one's ability to make choices will require an ability to question and criticize the dominant attitudes; and that too is an ability which has to be fostered by the right kind of education.

As with material conditions, so with cultural conditions, it is important to describe correctly the connection with freedom. Green's formulation is slightly ambiguous. 'Without a command of certain elementary arts and knowledge, the individual in modern society is as effectually crippled as by the loss of a limb or a broken constitution. He is not free to develop his faculties' (p. 373–4). The second sentence rather suggests that the connection between education and freedom is like the connection posited by Caudwell between material goods and freedom—that if education is made available to me, I am then free to acquire it, freedom thus being equated with getting what one wants. Green's first sentence comes closer to stating the true connection: that education and knowledge are conditions of freedom, enhancing one's ability to make choices.

So far, then, I have made the following claims about the concept of freedom. I have suggested that it is itself essentially a positive concept, denoting the ability to make choices. This in turn is closely connected with certain characteristic conditions, both negative and positive, which facilitate the making of choices. The negative condition is the absence of constraint or restriction—non-interference. The positive conditions are political powers, material goods, and cultural conditions such as education, knowledge, and understanding. I do not want to say that these are straightforwardly either necessary or sufficient conditions of freedom. 'Non-interference', I suppose, comes closest to being describable as a necessary condition, for an extreme degree of coercion or restriction could reasonably be said to deprive me of my freedom altogether. Political power, on the other hand, could certainly not be called a necessary condition of freedom, for I might totally lack all such institutionalized powers and yet still be able to make important choices about what to do with my own life. Clearly not one of the conditions could by itself be described as a sufficient condition, for the addition of any of the others would give me greater freedom. Neither, however, can they properly be described as jointly sufficient conditions, for that suggests a view of freedom as an all-or-nothing phenomenon—as though, once all these conditions were present, my freedom could be said to be complete. I do not in fact think that the notion of 'complete freedom' is an intelligible one. Rather, freedom is a matter of degree, and the extent of one's freedom depends on the extent to which these conditions are present.

The relation between freedom and its conditions is, then, a causal one. The conditions are not part of the definition of freedom, but the connection is a very close causal connection. The relevant factors are not just ones which may, on some occasions, happen to promote freedom; the connection is a constant one. Nor is the causal claim a contentious one, in the way that we might argue about whether violent revolutions, say, or industrialization, tend to increase or diminish freedom. Rather, these are the characteristic and standard conditions, the presence or absence of which will, in any human society, promote or limit freedom. And this is true in virtue of certain very basic facts about human beings and the nature of human action.

What now of Green's further claim—that 'freedom' is not only a 'positive' but also a 'social' concept? One version of this was:

(3) One can be free only in society.

The truth of this claim should now be apparent. It goes without saying that the political conditions of freedom would not be available outside society, but that is of no great import, since it could equally be said that outside society they would not be needed. More to the point is that the material conditions and the cultural conditions are created only by human social life. The scientific and technical control over the natural world, gradually accumulated over the centuries of human history, makes available to human beings an ever-increasing range of choices. And without the socially acquired command of language, and the activities of imagination and prediction which it makes possible, human beings could hardly be said to be capable of making choices at all. A human being brought up outside human society—raised by wolves, perhaps—might perhaps enjoy the kind of freedom which a wild animal has, but could not, except to a minimal degree, envisage alternatives and choose between them. What Green has to say about the 'wandering savage', then, is essentially correct.

Very different, however, is his claim (4): 'Freedom is the development and exercise of one's powers of contributing to social good.' This is not established by anything that we have been saying—or by anything else, as far as I can see. A human being living in a materially and culturally advanced society might thereby acquire an extensive ability to choose amongst a great variety of goods, yet direct that ability entirely to the limited pursuit of his or her own private good, neglecting the wider good of the society. I do not see why one should, on that account, describe such a person as any the less free.

More problematic is Green's claim (5): 'The development of the powers and capacities of some members of a society is not an advance towards the true freedom of man if it is denied to other members of that society.' In this formulation of Green's claim I have retained his evasive use of phrases such as 'advance to true freedom'. Evidently human beings may in some sense be free without exhibiting what Green would count as *true* freedom. Shorn of such evasive language, Green's claim amounts to the assertion that no one can be free unless everyone in his or her society is free, and that on the face of it looks exceedingly implausible. Surely the point about unfree societies is precisely that, in them, some people are free at the expense of the freedom of others. Nevertheless there are further arguments which we ought to look at which give some plausibility to Green's claim.

One such argument is the argument from the need for recognition. Here is a statement of it formulated by the nineteenth-century anarchist Michael Bakunin:

I am only properly free when all the men and women about me are equally free. . . . I only become truly free through the liberty of others, so that the more I am surrounded by free men, and the deeper and wider this freedom grows, the further my own extends. . . . I cannot truly call myself free until my liberty, in other words my dignity as a man, and my human right, which consists in not obeying any other man and behaving only in accordance with my own convictions, are reflected in the equally free awareness of all men and return to me confirmed by the assent of all the world.[2]

Like so much else in this chapter, the argument derives from Hegel, and specifically from his discussion of the master–slave relation in his *Phenomenology of Mind*. According to Hegel, the master requires from his slaves or servants not only service but also recognition and acknowledgement. He needs them to confirm his own power and dignity as a free agent. This requirement, however, is self-defeating. By the very fact that the master compels the slave to obey his orders, he can set no store by any recognition which he exacts from him. That recognition is not freely given; it is forced, compelled, and therefore not genuine. Genuine recognition could come only from another free man, from whom it could not be compelled. In short, I cannot be recognized as a free man unless I live in the company of other free men.[3]

Why should such recognition be necessary? Bakunin does not say. Hegel's explanation is characteristically obscure, but what it seems to come down to is this. My own view of myself can have no certainty, no objectivity, unless it is confirmed by others. Human behaviour is typically ambiguous, open to interpretation in different ways. If my own way of seeing myself is to count for anything, if I am to set any store by it, it must coincide with the way in which others see me.

This argument does have some force. There is indeed a certain futility in the actions of the lone tyrant, surrounded by fawning courtiers and abject slaves whose lavish praise he cannot take seriously. At best, however, it shows only that, to feel myself free, I need the company of *some* other free human beings. It does not show that *all* those around me must be equally free. It is consistent with the existence of slaves, or of an oppressed or exploited class, provided only that I do not depend on them for recognition. To take Green's example of the slave societies of antiquity, Bakunin's

---

[2] Michael Bakunin, *Selected Writings*, ed. Arthur Lehning (London 1973), p. 148.
[3] G. W. F. Hegel, *The Phenomenology of Mind*, trans. J. B. Baillie (London 1931), or the more recent version translated as *The Phenomenology of Spirit* by A. V. Miller (Oxford 1977), section B.IV.A. 'Independence and Dependence of Self-consciousness: Lordship and Bondage'.

argument could not support the claim that the freedom of the slave-owning citizens was not true freedom, since they could perfectly well be recognized as free by one another. Perhaps more far-reaching is the Marxist argument to which I have previously referred. Marx and Engels claim, as we have seen, that the level of freedom is largely determined by the growth of scientific and technical control over nature, that this growth is a social process and that therefore the freedom which it creates is a social rather than a purely individual acquisition. They also emphasize not only control over natural forces but control over social forces, and they believe that social forces become alienated and outside human control primarily because of divisions within a society—divisions between classes and divisions between individuals. In particular, in a capitalist economy where the owners of capital dominate those who own only their labour power, all are in turn dominated by the market, by the blind and uncontrollable market forces created by the competing activities of separate individuals and groups. Therefore even those who possess economic power are fundamentally unfree. This domination, according to the Marxist argument, can be ended only when economic life is brought under conscious and planned social control. Freedom, then, can be properly and fully possessed by individuals only when it is acquired by society as a whole.

The argument is a powerful one, but again I am not sure just how far it takes us. It does not, I think, support any simple claim to the effect that no one is free unless all are free. Though it asserts that in a class-divided society there are important respects in which no one is free, it also asserts that in other equally important respects some are freer than others. Moreover, there are difficulties in this notion of a universal freedom which consists in 'society openly and directly taking possession of the productive forces which have outgrown all control except that of society as a whole'.[4] What form, exactly, is this control by 'society as a whole' supposed to take? May it not mean, in practice, the central planning of economic life by some in the name of all? May it

<hr />

[4] Engels, *Anti-Dühring*, p. 331.

not therefore, though nominally a freedom exercised by the society as a whole, amount effectively to a freedom exercised by a limited group as a power over others? These are difficult questions, to which we shall return in due course. For the moment, however, it seems that the Marxist account is at least compatible with the existence, both in class societies and in a socialist society, of greater freedom for some than for others.

Neither Bakunin's argument nor the Marxist argument, then, are fully adequate to support Green's claim that a freedom enjoyed by some at the expense of others is not true freedom. On the other hand, they are at any rate sufficient to subvert Mill's model of freedom as something enjoyed by individuals in so far as they are left alone by society. The three categories of positive conditions which I have listed— political power, material resources, and cultural and educational resources—are all conditions which have to be socially created. They can be enjoyed by human beings only in so far as they share a common life in society.

We therefore have to seek some other solution to Mill's problem of the social distribution of freedom. The problem arises, we have seen, because people's freedoms conflict, and some way has therefore to be found of determining which freedoms should be sustained and which should be sacrificed. Mill's solution was that within the sphere of actions which affect only his or her own interests, the freedom of the individual must be sacrosanct, but that actions which affect the interests of others may properly be curtailed if they would do too much harm to others. We saw that the attempted demarcation between self-affecting and other-affecting actions breaks down in practice. We have now found, I believe, that the more fundamental theoretical division on which it rests, between the individual and society, is equally impossible to maintain.

This is not to say that Mill's demarcations are without value. They derive their plausibility from our sense that there is indeed a part of our lives which we properly regard as a 'private' realm. However, the notion of 'privacy' is distorted if it is held to belong only to activities in which we engage as individuals. The typical components of our 'private lives' are activities involving intimate relationships with other people—sexual relations, the life of the family, close personal friendships. We rightly feel that the intimacy of these activities would be destroyed if they were brought under the control of some larger public authority. That does not mean, however, that they constitute the only or even the most important sphere in which we exercise freedom, nor does it mean that they are activities in which we engage as individuals. They are social activities, and the distinction here is between small-scale and large-scale social relations.

When robbed of the plausibility which it derives from this notion of 'privacy', the individual–society dichotomy can be seen to be an inadequate tool for resolving the problem of the distribution of freedoms. Because freedom is created and fostered by social activities and institutions, we have, inescapably, to decide how those social activities and institutions are to be channelled and directed. When developed in one direction they may promote certain kinds of freedoms for some people, when developed in another direction they may promote other kinds of freedoms for others. The resultant dilemmas cannot be solved by Mill's criterion. When we consider practical issues such as state control of economic enterprises (as with the Factory Acts), or compulsory education, we need some more positive principle of distribution.

A natural candidate which then comes to mind is a principle of equality. If different social policies will produce different aggregations of freedom for different people, should we not adopt those policies which will result in an equal distribution of freedom to all? That, at any rate, is a widely held view. Properly formulated, it would be the principle that, other things being equal, we should aim at the promotion of the maximum amount of freedom compatible with an equal distribution of freedom—or, as it is sometimes put, everyone should have as much freedom as is compatible with the same degree of freedom for everyone else.

We are thus brought to a consideration of our second great political ideal—the ideal of equality. Our assessment of the principle of the equal distribution of freedom must depend upon an assessment of the validity of equality as a more general ideal. To that task I now turn.

# 4

## Arguments for Equality

THE concept of equality has a more contested status than that of freedom. The value of freedom is securely grounded in experience. Most people have known what it is to have their freedom limited or restricted, and have experienced it as a frustration and a loss. Most people have known circumstances in which they have experienced a sense of freedom, and it is something which they have valued. It is, as Mill rightly says, linked with a sense of using all one's faculties, one's powers of discrimination and judgement and decision, and of living one's life to the full. Politicians, not to mention advertisers, can exploit the connotations of 'freedom' and expect a ready response.

'Equality' does not have such resonances. With its mathematical connotations it looks more like an artificial ideal divorced from experience, and its adherents can the more easily be represented as dogmatic idealists attempting to impose an abstract scheme upon an untidy world. Whilst few can be found to reject the value of freedom, assessments of equality are more radically divided—hence my claim that there is a fundamental political division between those who seek to combine freedom and equality and those who reject equality in the name of freedom.

I shall aim to show in this chapter that, despite appearances, the value of equality is in fact grounded in experience. I shall look at some of the standard philosophical arguments which have been offered in defence of equality, and I shall suggest that they are unsatisfactory just in so far as they fail to do justice to those features of our experience which underlie the value of equality. I shall consider two sets of arguments, which I shall call 'formal' arguments and 'utilitarian' arguments, and I shall then seek to identify a form of argument which overcomes the contrasting limitations of those two sets.

It might be thought that, before attempting this task, I

ought to define more clearly just what it is that these arguments are supposed to be arguments for. 'Equality' seems to have not only a contested status but also an indeterminate content. If we value equality, what exactly is it that we value? Equality between whom? And in what respects do we want them to be equal? Is the suggestion that in all of our actions we should aim at promoting equality between all human beings in every respect, or is it a more limited ideal? Clearly these questions need to be answered, but I do not think that we can find answers until we have looked at the arguments in defence of equality. Different arguments will, if they work, justify different versions of the idea of equality, so only by considering which of these arguments are in fact valid can we decide what version of equality can be defended.

I shall look first, then, at a number of arguments which can all be classified as formal arguments, that is to say, arguments which appeal primarily to considerations of logic rather than to empirical considerations. I begin with one which makes no appeal to empirical facts or indeed to any facts at all: the suggestion that the requirement of equality needs no further justification. The idea here is one which has been referred to as the 'presumption of equality', the idea that it is unequal treatment of people that stands in need of justification. Inequalities, it is said, are arbitrary unless some reason is given for them; therefore, if no such reasons are forthcoming, it is rational to treat people equally. The suggestion here is not that no reasons for treating people unequally could ever be found. Rather, it is that the onus is on the advocate of inequality, rather than the advocate of equality, to supply reasons.[1]

Now it may be true, in some general sense, that inequalities are arbitrary if no reason can be given for them. However, it does not follow that equality is then any less arbitrary. All that follows is that, in the absence of reasons, *any* pattern of distribution, equal or unequal, is arbitrary. In other words, it does not matter what pattern of distribution is adopted.

[1] Cf. Isaiah Berlin, 'Equality', in *Proceedings of the Aristotelian Society* 1955–6, p. 303; S. I. Benn and R. S. Peters, *Social Principles and the Democratic State* (London 1959) p. 111; R. S. Peters, *Ethics and Education* (London 1966) p. 121.

Equality is just as arbitrary as inequality, unless some positive reason can be given for it. I do not see how, in the absence of such reasons, there can be any positive 'presumption of equality'.

The idea of a 'presumption of equality' can perhaps be made more plausible if it is linked with the idea of 'universalizability'.[2] Philosophers have made much of the claim that rational principles of action must be universalizable, that is, they must treat like cases alike. Consider an example which may seem to make plausible the connection with equality. Suppose that I give one of my children 50p pocket money. It may be said that, to be consistent, I should view my action as exemplifying a universal principle, and should therefore also give each of my other children 50p pocket money. To do so, then, would be to treat them equally. However, if we think further about this example, we can see that it does not really take us far in the direction of equality. Even if consistency requires that I give all my children 50p pocket money, it does not require that I give everyone 50p. In other words, there has to be some positive feature of the situation which entitles us to say that other cases are indeed 'like cases' and should therefore be treated alike. In the present example, the relevant positive feature is that the recipient is my child; that is why I give her pocket money, and that is why we can say that there is a positive presumption that I should give the other children pocket money. The mere requirement of universalizability does not, by itself, create any such positive presumption. Notice, secondly, that there may be very good reasons for giving my children unequal amounts of pocket money. I may give one child more because she is older, or because she is more helpful, or because she does better at school, or for any number of reasons. This is connected with the first point. The mere requirement of universalizability does not by itself create a positive presumption of equality. Whether there is such a presumption depends on the particular features of the case. They may be

---

[2] The idea of universalizability has been most fully developed by R. M. Hare; see especially his *Freedom and Reason* (Oxford 1963). Hare links universalizability with equality in his paper 'Justice and Equality' in J. Arthur and W. H. Shaw, (eds.), *Justice and Economic Distribution* (New Jersey 1978).

such as to make equal treatment appropriate—but then again, they may not. It all depends on the particular case.

In an attempt to strengthen the universalizability argument, it has been pointed out that not just anything can count as a relevant reason for treating people differently. The point has been made by Bernard Williams in an influential article on 'The Idea of Equality'.[3] According to Williams, a racist who urged that black people should be treated as inferior just because they are black would not thereby have given any *relevant* reason for treating blacks and whites unequally. The mere fact of the colour of a person's skin is not in itself a relevant reason for differential treatment, and someone who treated people differently solely on that basis would be simply irrational. Williams says:

This point is in fact conceded by those who practise such things as colour discrimination. Few can be found who will explain their practice merely by saying, 'But they're black: and it is my moral principle to treat black men differently from others.' If any reasons are given at all, they will be reasons that seek to correlate the fact of blackness with certain other considerations which are at least candidates for relevance to the question of how a man should be treated: such as insensitivity, brute stupidity, ineducable irresponsibility, etc. (p. 113)

Williams is right, I think; not just any fact, such as the colour of a person's skin, can be relevant to how that person should be treated. However, this still does not take us very far. As Williams's own remarks about racists indicate, there remain all sorts of reasons which could in principle be given for treating people unequally—that they are more or less intelligent than one another, more or less sensitive, and so on. The point is, again, that the requirement of universalizability does not create any positive presumption of equality, and therefore does not itself set any effective limits to the reasons which can be given for treating people unequally. Why, for example, should I not justify my favouring one person against others simply by saying that I like him? In the abstract this would seem to be as good a reason as any and, provided I apply it consistently, the argument from universalizability does nothing to rule it out of court.

If universalizability cannot by itself generate a positive presumption of equality, perhaps it can do so in conjunction with certain positive features of human beings which make like cases relevantly alike. Thus, for example, it has been suggested that the very fact that all human beings are human, vacuous though it may sound, is a relevant ground for equal treatment. This suggestion too has been advocated by Williams, who says:

That all men are human is, if a tautology, a useful one, serving as a reminder that those who belong anatomically to the species *homo sapiens* . . . are also alike in certain other respects more likely to be forgotten. These respects are notably the capacity to feel pain, both from immediate physical causes and from various situations represented in perception and in thought; and the capacity to feel affection for others, and the consequences of this, connected with the frustration of this affection, loss of its objects, etc. (p. 112)

A little later Williams adds that, as well as the capacity to feel pain and the desire for affection, another important feature of human beings is the desire for self-respect, which he elaborates as 'a certain human desire to be identified with what one is doing, to be able to realize purposes of one's own, and not to be the instrument of another's will unless one has willingly accepted such a role' (p. 114). The relevance of all this to equality is that if we treat some people as though they lacked these characteristics, and neglect the claims which arise from them, we are neglecting features which they share with all other human beings, and in that sense we are treating people unequally.

This argument again seems to me to be too weak. In the first place, one may in a perfectly straightforward sense recognize that all human beings share these features, without thereby accepting that one has obligations to all human beings to minister to these needs in them. To take an extreme case, the sadist certainly does not neglect the fact that people have a capacity to feel pain; he could hardly be a sadist if he did. Less dramatically, one may recognize that everyone needs to avoid pain, and to give and be given affection, and to feel self-respect, but hold that one has obligations to try to satisfy these needs only for a limited circle of people, and that outside that circle such needs are other people's responsibility.

Furthermore, even if I make some attempt to avoid causing pain to anyone, and pay some regard to the basic human needs of everyone, and avoid treating anyone as a mere instrument of my will, this may still fall a long way short of treating people as equals. To require that everyone be treated as human, even in the positive sense, is to require merely that a basic moral decency be observed, and that no one should be degraded and treated as of no account; it is perfectly compatible with some people being better off than others in all sorts of ways.

Given that the truism 'All human beings are human' does not take us far enough, one further variation which may be played on the universalizability theme is the truism 'All interests are interests'. The suggestion here is that, to be consistent, we must regard the interests of all persons as equally important. If I recognize that I have good reason to be concerned for the interests of one person, then I ought logically to recognize that the equivalent interests of other persons are just as much interests, and that therefore I have just as good a reason to be concerned for them. Indeed, consistency requires that I show equal concern for the interests not only of all persons, but of all beings which have interests, that is, of all sentient beings. Thus we arrive at the principle of equality which has been called the principle of 'equal consideration of interests'.[4]

The difficulties with this suggestion are in part the same as those with the previous candidate. I can recognize that all interests are interests, without thereby being committed to the belief that the appropriate response on my part is to try to satisfy those interests. More importantly, in those cases where I *am* concerned for someone's interests, this may be not just because the interests are interests, but because of the

---

[4] Stanley I. Benn, 'Egalitarianism and the Equal Consideration of Interests', in J. Roland Pennock and John W. Chapman, (eds.), *Nomos IX: Equality* (New York 1967), and in Bedau, *Justice and Equality*. Peter Singer, *Practical Ethics* (Cambridge 1979), ch.2.

particular nature of the person or the particular nature of my relation to that person. I may, for example, have a particular concern for someone because that person is my friend. This may, perhaps, logically commit me to exhibiting the same concern for anyone else with whom I have as close a friendship; but it certainly does not commit me to exhibiting the same concern for every sentient being. Any notion of equality which was thought to carry that implication would have to deny the ethical significance of any of the specific kinds of relations in which we stand to one another: ties of affection, family ties, all the manifold kinds of social and institutional relationships. That version of equality seems to me to be a nonsense.

Even if the principle of equal consideration of interests were acceptable, it would still not be a principle of equality in any very strong sense. All it says is that the same interests should always carry the same weight, regardless of whose interests they are. That, however, does not mean that the outcome will be the equal satisfaction of everybody's interests, that is, an outcome in which everyone benefits equally. It would, for example, in principle be compatible with the justifying of a slave society, built on a fundamental inequality between the slaves and their owners. Though the slaves might suffer from this arrangement, it might be that their suffering is simply outweighed by the very great benefits derived by the slaveowners. It is not that the slaves' interests are not being taken into account, it is just that there are not enough of them for their interests to outweigh those of the slaveowners. Each person may count equally in the weighing process, but a larger number of substantial interests in one pan of the scales will outweigh a smaller number of equally substantial interests in the other pan. In short, what the principle of equal consideration of interests amounts to is not a genuine principle of equality, but a version of utilitarianism. Everybody's interests count equally, but the aim is simply to maximize the satisfaction of those interests, regardless of how the satisfaction is distributed.

Mention of utilitarianism may, at this point, prompt us to change to a completely different tack. All the arguments we have looked at so far are essentially formal arguments. A typical utilitarian is likely to comment that of course mere formal considerations will by themselves yield no ethical conclusion. A principle of equality, like any other ethical principle, has to be justified not by mere logic, but by an appeal to facts about the world. Certainly utilitarianism could in principle justify great inequalities. Nevertheless we could, from a utilitarian point of view, justify equality if we could show that in practice equality is likely to do more good than inequality. In other words, we would have to show that, given the way the world is, egalitarian social arrangements are likely to yield greater benefits overall than alternative sets of social arrangements.[5]

Two facts about the world, in particular, have regularly been invoked in utilitarian arguments for equality. One is the fact of what is called 'diminishing marginal utility'. The idea here is that the more you have of something, the less benefit you gain from acquiring even more of it. Suppose that you and I each own a house. They are similar houses and we benefit more or less equally from them. Suppose now that I acquire your house from you, leaving you homeless. I may be somewhat better off than I was. I have more space to make use of, and with two houses to choose from I can enjoy a change of scene when I feel like it. You, however, will be much worse off, for you will have to suffer all the hardships of homelessness. From a utilitarian point of view, then, my gain will almost certainly be outweighed by your loss. It would therefore seem that if there are two houses available for two people, more good can be produced overall if each person has one house than if one person has both houses. In other words, the egalitarian arrangement is to be preferred to the inegalitarian one on grounds of utility. Moreover, if I go on and on acquiring houses, I am likely to benefit less and less from them. My second house is of less benefit to me than my first, but my sixteenth house is likely to be of very little benefit to me at all. It would seem, then, that the greater the inequalities, the less the overall benefit gained from the resources available.

[5] Utilitarian arguments for equality are explored by Hare, 'Justice and Equality', and by Singer, *Practical Ethics*. Hare's support for equality is cautious, Singer's is more vigorous.

The second fact commonly invoked in utilitarian arguments for equality is the fact of envy. If people are aware that others have more than they do, they may well feel envious. This envy will in itself be a source of unhappiness for the people who feel it. It may also lead them to do other things which create further unhappiness, ranging from expressing their bitterness and resentment to forcibly seizing the property of those who have more. It therefore seems plausible to suppose that a good deal of discontent, antagonism, and social instability can be avoided by greater equality.

Let us take this second factual claim first. It is empirically contestable. People can be, and often are, reconciled to inequalities, especially if they think that the inequalities are justifiable. But this in turn points us to a much more important and more fundamental defect in the argument. Whether or not people resent inequalities depends in part on whether they believe that those inequalities are justified. If the resentment arises from a sense that the inequalities are unjustified, it is misrepresented by the 'argument from envy'. That argument then inverts the proper relation between resentment and inequality. It says that too much inequality is wrong because it makes people feel resentment. What should be said, however, is that people feel resentment at inequalities because they believe that inequality is wrong. Their resentment is not just a feeling of envy, it is not just a perverse resentment of other people's success. They themselves would regard it as an ethically justified response, because of their antecedent ethical belief that inequality is wrong. They would claim, perhaps, that they have a right to equal treatment, and that the existence of inequality is an injustice committed against them. It is for such reasons that they feel resentment. The argument from envy, then, cannot account for this antecedent ethical belief.

Essentially the same objections apply to the argument from diminishing marginal utility. Again, the argument cannot make sense of the idea that inequality is an injustice against those who are treated unequally, the idea that people have a valid ethical claim to equal treatment. The argument from diminishing marginal utility says that inequality is wrong because it diminishes the overall quantity of happiness or welfare. It says nothing about the idea that specific people are wronged by this inequality, and are wronged because they are thereby treated unjustly. Inequality, if it is wrong, is a wrong done to those who are treated in this way. It is not wrong simply because of its further effects on the sum of human happiness.

At this point let us take stock of the arguments we have reviewed so far. Both sets of arguments, the formal arguments and the utilitarian arguments, fail, it seems to me, because they do not match up to our sense of what is important about equality. What we find objectionable about inequality is not any shortcoming in logic, a failure to be consistent, yet that is what the formal arguments would imply. By contrast the utilitarian arguments do at least have the merit of locating the wrongness of inequality in certain empirical facts about the nature of inequality. They err, however, in focusing on external facts, facts about the further consequences of equality and inequality. Equality is important not just because of what it leads to, but because of what it *is*.

What is it, then? The term 'equality' refers to the way in which people are properly to be treated. They are to be treated in that way because they are entitled to such treatment, because such treatement is just. 'Equality', then, is to be understood as a particular version of the idea of 'justice'. Utilitarians have struggled to provide a satisfactory account of justice. (Mill, for example, devotes to that task the final chapter of his essay *Utilitarianism*.) They have failed because they have treated the idea of justice as derivative rather than as fundamental. Utilitarianism is an aggregative theory; it tells us that we should be primarily concerned with how much good is done overall, and only secondarily concerned with the question of distribution, the question of who gets what. For a utilitarian, one distribution of goods is to be preferred to another only if it increases the overall amount of good. There is no room here for the idea that a certain distribution of goods is to be preferred because it is in itself right and proper. Utilitarianism ignores the ethical significance of the fact that people stand in particular relations to one another, and that those relations make a particular distribution of goods appropriate. What we need, then, is an argument for equality which seeks to present it as a plausible interpretation of the idea of justice, and which in turn seeks to ground the idea of justice in certain kinds of social relations. What form might such an argument take?

The most influential egalitarian argument of this kind is the theory of justice expounded by the contemporary American philosopher John Rawls.[6] Rawls's theory is not a defence of pure equality, and I shall say something later about his departure from simple equality. Nevertheless, his position is in a broad sense an egalitarian one, and it is in that guise that I want to consider it.

Rawls's theory makes use of the idea, popular with many seventeenth- and eighteenth-century political philosophers, of a 'social contract'. Traditional 'social contract' theory (which I shall discuss again in chapter 7) describes human beings existing in a 'state of nature' without any social institutions, and then coming together to make a contract which will set up an organized society. In place of the problematic notion of a 'state of nature' Rawls asks us to imagine human beings in what he calls 'the original position'. These people come together to decide on principles of justice which are to govern their subsequent dealings with one another as a community. We are to envisage that, in choosing their principles of justice, each will decide as a rationally self-interested being, capable of calculating what set of principles is most likely to promote his or her own interests. They are, however, to make their choice from behind a veil of ignorance. They do not know what position they will occupy in the community. If some of them are going to end up better off than others, none of them knows in advance whether he or she will be one of the privileged or one of the underprivileged. They do not know what particular talents and abilities they will have. It would therefore be rash for any of them to accept, for instance, a principle allotting the greatest rewards to the most intelligent, since none of them knows whether he

---

[6] Rawls's theory is set out in full in his book *A Theory of Justice* (Oxford 1972). A more manageable introduction to the theory is his earlier article 'Justice as Fairness' in *Philosophical Review* 67 (1958), reprinted in Laslett and Runciman, *Philosophy, Politics and Society*, and in Bedau, *Justice and Equality*. There are useful selections from *A Theory of Justice* in Arthur and Shaw, *Justice and Economic Distribution*.

or she will be one of the most intelligent. They do not even know what particular vision of the good life they will each be pursuing, and hence they are in no position to propose, in their own interests, that any particular goods should be provided in greater abundance than others.

Rawls suggests that rationally self-interested beings in the original position would choose the following two principles of justice:

(i) Each person is to have an equal right to the most extensive basic liberty compatible with a similar liberty for others.

(ii) Social and economic inequalities are to be arranged so that (a) they are to the greatest benefit of the least advantaged, and (b) they are attached to offices and positions open to all under conditions of fair equality of opportunity.

As I have said, these are not principles of pure equality, but they are markedly egalitarian in so far as they stipulate that liberty is to be shared equally by all, opportunities are to be equal, and other goods are to be distributed equally unless everyone, including the least well-off, would benefit more from an unequal distribution. Rawls's claim is, then, that rationally self-interested individuals in the original position would choose these principles. Other, less egalitarian principles might turn out to benefit them more, but from behind the veil of ignorance they cannot know this, because they do not know where they will end up. These principles will ensure that either they are as well off as everyone else or, if they are less well off than some others, at any rate they are better off than they would otherwise have been, since inequalities have to benefit everyone.

Rawls's theory has generated an enormous volume of discussion, and I have nothing new to add to it, but I want to endorse two criticisms which have frequently been made. Both criticisms concern his use of a version of social contract theory. In the first place it is questionable whether rational, self-interested individuals in the original position would in fact choose Rawls's two principles. Whether they would do so would depend on how bold they were as risk-takers. If they were cautious, they might indeed hedge their bets in the way which Rawls thinks would lead to his two principles. They might, however, be willing to gamble; they might, for instance, opt for principles which allotted special privileges to the strongest or to the most intelligent. In the original position they would not know whether they would turn out to be among the strongest or the most intelligent; but if they did turn out to be so, they would have gained from the gamble, and if they did not, they might still feel that it is better to have gambled and lost than never to have gambled at all.

The second criticism relates to Rawls's insistence that the social contract in his theory is a purely hypothetical one, not an actual historical event. In saying this he avoids notorious difficulties in traditional social contract theory (difficulties to which I shall refer again in chapter 7). However, he does so only at the cost of leaving it quite unclear what relevance this hypothetical contract can have to our actual circumstances. We have none of us actually made such a contract, so why should we act as though we were bound by it? In particular, we are not in the original position. We know what place in society we presently occupy, what our natural assets and abilities are, what our conception of the good is. Even if it were true, then, that Rawls's two principles are the ones which we would adopt in the original position, why should our dealings be governed by them when we are *not* in the original position?

I would want, then, to criticize each of the two main components in Rawls's contract theory: the appeal to rational self-interest, and the appeal to a hypothetical original position characterized by a veil of ignorance. Rawls says of these two components: '. . . the combination of mutual disinterest and the veil of ignorance achieves the same purpose as benevolence. For this combination of conditions forces each person in the original position to take the good of others into account' (*A Theory of Justice* p. 148). It is precisely this conception of the theory that I want to contest. It seems to me that the combination of rational self-interest and the veil of ignorance does not in fact do what Rawls claims for it.

As I have said, there is nothing original about these criticisms, but I make them because I now want to distinguish two conflicting strands in Rawls's theory: the strand which I have just criticized, and a strand which seems to me to be valid and important. These two strands can be labelled, respectively, 'justice as contract' and 'justice as co-operation'. The first is the idea that principles of justice are those which would be chosen by rationally self-interested individuals from behind a veil of ignorance. It seems to me to be misguided. The second is the idea which Rawls expresses as follows:

> The intuitive idea is that since everyone's well-being depends upon a scheme of cooperation without which no one could have a satisfactory life, the division of advantages should be such as to draw forth the willing cooperation of everyone taking part in it, including those less well situated. (Ibid. p. 15)

In short, the principles of justice are principles appropriate to a co-operative organization, because they are principles on which everyone committed to such co-operation can agree.

This idea, though present in Rawls's theory, is distorted by being linked with the idea of a hypothetical contract. I want now to detach it from that context and attempt to develop it further. I will begin with a simple example. Consider a group of people coming together in some joint enterprise. Imagine, for instance, a number of people who have decided to share a house, and who have to decide on the apportioning of the tasks necessary to keep the house in good order—who is to do the cleaning, who is to do the cooking, and so on. We do not have to imagine, in the manner of Rawls, that they decide on their arrangements from behind a veil of ignorance. We need only assume that they are genuinely and fully committed to working in co-operation. How, then, will they make their decision?

I want to suggest that two things follow from their commitment to co-operation. First, this will affect the way in which they make their decision. It will be a joint decision, not one imposed by some of them on the others. Everyone will be able to have their say. If possible, they will try to agree on a decision acceptable to all of them. If they cannot reach an agreement, they will at any rate make sure that everyone's view is taken into account. This means that if, in the end, they have to decide by voting, everyone will have an equal vote. But it also means that voting will not be used by a majority of the group to exploit a minority. If all the members of the group are committed to working together co-operatively, they will see to it that everyone's interests are taken into account and no one's interests are sacrificed to those of others. Interests may sometimes clash, and difficult decisions may have to be made, but they will be made in such a way that each person's commitment to the group is respected and not exploited.

In saying this we are already turning our attention from the way in which the decision is made to what is decided. This is the second thing which follows from the commitment to co-operation. The set of arrangements which is adopted by the group must be one which can be justified to each of its members. If a co-operative group is one in which each person has an equal say, then each of them can make an equal claim on the group; those claims, therefore, can be properly satisfied only by a state of affairs in which all benefit equally overall. We could think of this as something like what Rousseau calls 'the general will'. Each person's individual will, says Rousseau, is merged in the general will.[7] That makes it sound like a metaphysical abstraction, but it does not have to be. It corresponds to a real feature of our experience. When a number of people are fully committed to working together as a co-operative group, their deliberations take the form not of each person asking himself or herself 'How can I get the others to organize things in the way that I want?', but of their jointly asking 'How shall *we* organize things?' The first-person plural 'we' gives expression to a

---

[7] 'Each of us puts his person and all his power in common under the supreme direction of the general will, and, in our corporate capacity, we receive each member as an indivisible part of the whole.' (Jean-Jacques Rousseau, *The Social Contract* Book I, ch. 6.) 'The social compact sets up among the citizens an equality of such a kind, that they all bind themselves to observe the same conditions and should therefore all enjoy the same rights. Thus, from the very nature of the compact, every act of Sovereignty, i.e. every authentic act of the general will, binds or favours all the citizens equally . . .' (ibid. Book II, ch. 4). Although I invoke Rousseau here, I am not endorsing the details of his account.

general will in which each individual will participates equally; therefore the rational choice of that general will would be the choice of a situation in which each member benefits equally.

This still sounds rather abstract. Let us try to make it more concrete by developing the description of the members of our imaginary household apportioning the various tasks. They will not necessarily decide that each of them should participate equally in every task. It may be that some of them have special skills and abilities. One of them may have a particular flair for decorating, another may be a particularly good cook, and so on. They may decide to make full use of these skills by arranging for the relevant individuals to concentrate on what they are good at. Again, some may have particular handicaps or disabilities. One of them, perhaps, might be crippled and therefore unable to help with the cleaning, but might instead, say, take on the responsibility for keeping the household accounts. Or particular tasks might be especially inconvenient for some of them. One of them, for example, might have further to travel home from work and therefore not be able conveniently to help with preparing the evening meal. Their co-operating as a group need not prevent them from taking due account of all these complicating factors. What it will mean, however, is that they will do so in such a way that everyone benefits equally overall. And since, in this particular example, the benefits are primarily collective benefits—a clean and comfortable house, well-cooked meals, and so on—rather than individual goods which can be separately shared out, the notion of everyone's benefitting equally will in practice mean that everyone carries an equal share of the burdens necessary for producing these collective goods. No one benefits disproportionately by enjoying the collective benefits plus the additional benefit of not having to contribute their share of time and effort.

Such a set-up, then, is appropriate to a co-operative group because it is one which can be rationally justified to each of the participants. Suppose, now, that one of the members were to refuse to contribute an equal share, not by pleading some special disability for which he could compensate in some other way, but simply by saying something like 'I hate cleaning, I don't see why I should do it'. How could he justify his refusal to the rest of the group? Or suppose that the group were to decide that one of its members should do a greater share of the work than the rest. How could they justify this to him or her? Any such claim or any such imposition would radically alter the character of the group, so that it was no longer an authentically co-operative one.

Equality, then, will be a feature both of the way in which our co-operative group makes its decision, and of what it decides. These two aspects of equality can be formalized as two principles of justice. A conception of justice is a view about how things should be distributed within a group of people.[8] Two kinds of distribution are involved. First, any human group will involve a certain distribution of power. Here we are using the term 'distribution' in a rather wide or loose sense. When we talk about 'the distribution of power', we do not mean that 'power' is some independently identifiable commodity which can then be parcelled out in various ways. It is not that people are constituted as some kind of group or community, and then have to decide how this item called 'power' is going to be shared out among them; rather, the distribution of power determines the nature of the group itself, the nature of the relations which constitute it as a certain kind of community.

This community, constituted by power-relations of one sort or another, will engage in various activities to produce various goods. Questions of distribution of a second kind then arise—of distribution in the narrower sense. The goods which are produced must be distributed among the members of the group, and so must the responsibility for performing the activities necessary to produce them. Different people will have to engage in different, more or less onerous activities, and will acquire different goods as a result. We can call this the question of the distribution of benefits and burdens.

Principles of justice, then, are applied to these two questions, and specify how power, and benefits and burdens,

---

[8] Strictly speaking this is true only of what is called 'distributive justice'. The term 'justice' also has other applications, for instance 'legal justice'. Common to all the uses of 'justice' is the very general notion of persons receiving the appropriate treatment.

should rightly be distributed. From my discussion of the household example I have tried to show that the members of a community, if they are committed to co-operation with one another, will be guided by egalitarian principles of justice: (a) that power should be shared equally and (b) that benefits and burdens should be so distributed that everyone benefits equally overall.[9]

These two principles could, of course, conflict with one another. The members of the co-operative community, exercising power equally, might themselves decide to distribute benefits unequally. I shall consider in a moment some of the reasons which they might be thought to have for doing so. Certainly we cannot rule out in advance the possibility that there might be such reasons. What I want to suggest, however, is that in the absence of overriding reasons to the contrary it would be rational for them to distribute benefits and burdens so that everyone benefits equally. We can usefully re-introduce here an idea which we looked at earlier, that of a 'presumption of equality'. I criticized this idea at the beginning of this chapter, but now, in this new context, we can see why there should be a presumption of equality. In the abstract, there is no such presumption; but in the context of a co-operative group or community, there is a presumption of equality in the distribution of benefits and burdens, because that is part of what it is for the institution to be a co-operative one.

I have deliberately illustrated my argument with a very simple example. In the subsequent discussion in this and the following chapters we shall have to deal with the complexities which arise when we consider, for instance, a larger community, or one which involves the exercise of highly specialized skills, or when we consider the interaction

---

[9] For brevity's sake I shall refer to the second principle as 'equality of benefits and burdens', and sometimes, for even greater brevity, as 'equality of benefits'. I should therefore emphasize at this point that what I am talking about is equality in net benefit overall, i.e. that everyone benefits equally overall when the particular benefits which each member receives and the particular contributions with which each member is burdened are all taken into account.

The relationship between my two principles is formally analogous to the relation between Rawls's two principles of justice. Like Rawls I would claim that the first principle takes precedence over the second, for reasons which will become apparent in due course in chapter 6.

between different communities. What I want to suggest, however, and what I hope the subsequent discussions will confirm, is that the complexities can be dealt with by building on the simple model. They do not invalidate it, they only require us to add to it. I would claim that my argument for equality rests not on particular features of the simple example, but on the connection between equality and the very idea of co-operation. We can perhaps see the strength of this claim if we now look more closely at the meaning of the term 'co-operation'.

In a wide sense, 'co-operation' can refer to any interaction or association between a number of people producing a result which they could not have produced individually. In this sense it covers a wide range of relations between people, and has no necessary connection with equality. Notoriously, someone may be threatened, beaten up, tortured, and then asked 'Now will you co-operate?'—and of course the terms of such co-operation are highly unequal. I think we should say, however, that co-operation brought about in this way was not genuine co-operation. Our imagined gangster or torturer who asks 'Now will you co-operate?' can be regarded as employing the term with a certain degree of irony. I want to distinguish, therefore, between co-operation in the wide sense, for which I shall use the term 'association', and the narrower and stricter sense for which I shall reserve the term 'co-operation'.

There are forms of association, then, which are not genuinely co-operative. As our gangster example illustrates, what is distinctive of genuine co-operation is that it is freely entered into. Co-operation is a form of association in which people work together voluntarily, respecting one another as free participants in a common enterprise. This understanding of co-operation is confirmed by the way in which we contrast a co-operative community with other forms of association. Most obviously, a co-operative community is contrasted with a coercive form of association. A community of slaves and slave-owners may, for example, be able to achieve feats of productive activity which would have been impossible without this combining of the directing activity of the slave-owners and the physical labour of the slaves. For all that, it cannot be called a genuinely co-operative achievement. It is not one in which the slaves are freely engaged. Hence they and the slave-owners cannot be said to have co-operated with one another. The one group is merely used by the other.

We might, secondly, contrast a co-operative community with an exploitative one. In its clearest form exploitation is simply an extension of coercion. If the association between group A and group B is such that A uses its coercive power over B in order to promote its own interests at the expense of B's interests, that is a classic case of exploitation. In calling it 'exploitation' we add to the fact of coercion the fact of the differential satisfaction of interests. However, not every situation in which X's interests are promoted more effectively than Y's is a case of exploitation. If X and Y are neighbouring farmers and X, being a better farmer, prospers more than Y, that is not exploitation. It becomes such only if X prospers at the expense of Y, and that must mean that X prospers more than Y because of the nature of the association between them and because of the use which X makes of that association. X's prospering must be the cause of Y's doing less well than he might have done. It must also be the case, I think, that the use which X makes of that association to further his own interests must be at least partly deliberate, and that it must be something which Y has not freely and consciously accepted. The simplest way in which this can come about, then, is through X's having coercive power over Y, but other ways are possible. In particular, there is the familiar situation which we describe as 'exploiting other people's good will'. A number of people may be purportedly committed to acting in co-operation with one another, but some of them may fail to pull their weight. They may grab all the available advantages of co-operation, but default on their own contribution. They would then properly be described as exploiting the others and, as such, failing to co-operate.

One other standard contrast is between co-operation and competition. Here the contrast is less straightforward. There *is* a contrast. A competitive form of association is one in which some people do better than others, and, in a sense, do better at the expense of others, since the rewards are limited and if some people gain them, others are thereby excluded from them. Typically, also, the participants deliberately aim to do better than one another. So far there is a clear contrast with a co-operative form of association, whose participants aim to succeed or fail together. However, competition differs from exploitation in this respect: a competitive system is one in which the differences in rewards are institutionalized, and people may voluntarily participate in that institutional structure, knowing that some of them will do better than others. In other words, people may co-operate in a competitive system.

Here, then, we have a case where co-operation and equality seem to come apart. However, I think it would more properly be described as a case where the two egalitarian principles come apart, in the way that I have already anticipated. I have said that, from a position of equal power, people might freely agree to a system of unequal rewards. Co-operation in a competitive system would be an instance of this. We shall have to consider—and I shall do so shortly—what reasons the members of a co-operative community, sharing power equally, might have for sharing benefits unequally, and in particular for allotting benefits competitively. But even if there were good reasons, there would still remain the connection between co-operation and equality of power. If the latter were removed, we would be back with a situation in which some people did better than others because they had more power. That would be not just a competitive but an exploitative system, and the clear contrast with co-operation would re-emerge.

Leaving aside for the moment, then, the possibility of co-operative participation in a competitive system offering unequal rewards, I suggest that when we consider what co-operation is contrasted with, we can see more clearly the connection between co-operation and equality. Now it may be objected that I have made the connection all too clear— that I have simply defined a co-operative community by contrasting it with a community based on inequality. If that were so, I would have provided no real arguments for equality. My argument is that principles of equality are the principles of justice appropriate to a co-operative community. If it turns out that by a co-operative community I simply mean an egalitarian community, we shall have made no real progress. The task of arguing for equality will simply have been reformulated as the task of arguing for co-operation, and the difference between the two will be purely verbal.

I do not think that this is the situation we are in, however. My initial definition of a co-operative community did not itself make use of the concept of equality. I suggested that a co-operative community was a form of association in which people relate to one another as free participants in a common enterprise. The argument thus moves from the idea of co-operation, understood as an association of free individuals, to the idea of equality. That the argument takes this form is clearly important for the central theme of this book, the relation between freedom and equality, and I shall take up the point again in due course.

The second important feature of the argument is that it defends the relatively abstract idea of equality by reference to the more concrete idea of co-operation. In other words, I argue for equality by locating it in its social context. That is the great difference between my account, on the one hand, and the formal and utilitarian arguments on the other. My account, I would claim, properly reflects our sense of *why* equality is important. It grounds the idea of equality in the relevant features of human experience. The value of equality is the value of co-operative relations between people. That is why equality matters. Inequality is wrong because it violates the requirements of such relations, it is a betrayal of the relationship of co-operation. By linking equality with co-operation we also identify its proper application. It is not, as the formal arguments would imply, an entirely abstract and universal value applicable to all the dealings of human beings with one another. As we have seen, there are all sorts of specific human relationships where the requirement of equality is out of place. We rightly give a special importance to friends or lovers or family, because that is the nature of these special relationships. Equality however has its own proper place. Equality is the virtue appropriate to co-operative institutions, just because they are co-operative, and it is as such that we properly value it.

Rawls's theory of justice, we saw, is superior to the formal and utilitarian arguments because it takes more account of the need to argue for equality in social terms. It does so only half-heartedly, however. We can see this if we return to my contrast between the two strands in Rawls's theory, 'justice as contract' and 'justice as co-operation'. 'Justice as contract' is the dominant strand. It combines the ideas of 'individual self-interest' and the 'veil of ignorance'. Both these ideas prevent the contract argument from being a fully social argument. For all the talk of 'contract', the principles of egalitarian justice are not really presented as principles on which people agree. The appeal is to the interests of the individual, and the argument attempts to show that the principles would be chosen by any rationally self-interested individual calculating independently from behind the veil of ignorance. By contrast, the idea of 'justice as co-operation', when separated from the contract argument, no longer needs to demonstrate that principles of equality would be chosen on grounds of individual self-interest. It is indeed in people's interests to participate in co-operative activities; that is important, and I shall say more about its significance later. However, though people may share in co-operative activities for reasons of self-interest, their participation in such activities involves ceasing to think primarily in terms of purely individual self-interest. A crucial notion which I have invoked is that of 'commitment'. To enter into co-operative relations with others is, I have suggested, to commit oneself to the point of view of the shared project, it is to replace the question 'What will benefit me?' with the question 'What will benefit us?'. That is not to say that my concern for my own interests is irrevocably abandoned. If I find that the other participants in the enterprise are in fact exploiting me—if, that is, they are not treating me as an equal—then I may appropriately revert to a consideration of my own interests as an individual, and question my commitment to the enterprise; but that is because it has ceased to be a genuinely co-operative one.

The other factor which prevents Rawls's contract argument from being a fully social argument is its appeal to hypothetical considerations. The principles of justice are said to be principles which would be chosen by rational choosers in the entirely hypothetical 'original position' characterized by a 'veil of ignorance'. My own argument, in contrast, says that egalitarian principles are the principles appropriate to the actual co-operative institutions in which we are involved. These co-operative institutions may be of many varying kinds, they may range from the household of my earlier example to a whole society, but in so far as they are co-operative institutions, the principles appropriate to them are principles of equality.

In the remainder of this chapter I want to return to the consideration of a problem which I identified earlier. I said that the principles of 'equal power' and 'equal benefit' might come into conflict. The members of a co-operative community, exercising equal power, might freely decide upon an unequal distribution of benefits and burdens. That being so, the principle of equal benefit must have the status of a presumption of equality: in the absence of overriding reasons for an unequal distribution, it is rational for members of a co-operative community to distribute benefits and burdens so that everyone benefits equally overall. We have now to consider whether there are, in fact, good reasons which could override the presumption of equality.

In one sense the status of equality is, in this respect, the same as that of any other ethical principle. Since there is, I would maintain, an irreducible plurality of different ethical values, it is always possible that, in a particular situation, one value may come into conflict with another, and that one will then have to override the other. The value of respect for human life, for example, is as fundamental as any, but in extreme cases it may be necessary to kill for the sake of some other overwhelming good. Likewise we cannot rule out the possibility that equality may sometimes be outweighed by other values, nor can we anticipate all the possible conflicts which might arise. What we can do, however—and this is where there is a special problem for equality—is to consider other general principles of justice which might be thought to carry greater weight than the presumption of equality. If they do carry greater weight, then it would follow that equality must be overridden not just in special cases but as a matter of general principle. I shall therefore examine some alternative principles of justice which are commonly invoked to justify departures from equality. I shall try to show that some of these principles are themselves further elaborations of the idea of equality, and that those which are not egalitarian are in fact untenable.

Consider first the principle 'To each according to his need'. In one sense this ranks people very unequally, since some people's needs are much greater than others. A standard example is that of health care. Someone who is chronically sick, or permanently physically handicapped, will need a much greater share of medical resources than the normal healthy person. Nevertheless I would suggest that the underlying idea is one of equality. The aim is that everybody should, as far as possible, have an equally worthwhile life, and if some people have special needs, then they should be given special resources to pull them up as much as possible to the level of others. This is the reason why people's differing needs ought to be taken into account. Hence what looks at first like an inegalitarian principle turns out not to be, after all, a way of rebutting the presumption of equality.

Consider now another commonly invoked principle: 'To each according to his work'. This can, I think, be interpreted in two different ways. It may be understood as a principle of compensation. If some people work longer hours than others, for instance, or do especially dangerous or demanding work, they should get special rewards. The idea here is that special burdens have to be compensated for in order that those who have to bear these burdens can enjoy the same overall level of benefit as everyone else. Again, then, the underlying requirement is that of equality. Indeed, such a principle of compensation is central to the very idea of 'equal benefit' as I have previously formulated it.

However, the principle 'To each according to his work' may also be understood as meaning 'To each according to his merit'; in other words, those people who exhibit special skills or abilities deserve greater rewards. This is undeniably a negation of the principle of equality, an attempted justification of greater benefits for some than for others. To many people it is the very essence of justice—that people should get what they deserve. Here, then, we have an important rival to egalitarian ideas of justice.

One possible rejoinder to it is that what abilities one inherits are not one's own doing, they are a matter of luck, and if one is lucky enough to have special skills and abilities that is no reason why one should be further favoured with special rewards.[10] Still, it may be replied, though one's possession of special abilities is a matter of luck, what one does with those abilities is not a matter of luck, it is one's own doing and as such it is something which can appropriately be rewarded. If one has used one's abilities to make a specially valuable contribution to the community, then one deserves more.

What, then, are we to make of this idea of 'desert' or 'merit'?[11] I suggest that, to answer this question, we need to distinguish the pure idea of 'desert' from other closely-related notions. There is first the idea of 'compensation' which I have already mentioned and which I have said is itself equality-based. The idea that people should be compensated with benefits in proportion to the burdens which they undertake, so as to bring everyone up to the same level of benefit overall, could reasonably be described as a notion of 'rewarding' people for their contributions. There is a crucial difference, however, between this and the strict notion of reward for desert. Essential to the idea of compensation is that what people are compensated for must be describable as, in some sense, a 'burden'. This does not mean that it necessarily has to be actively painful or unpleasant. Consider the classic case of work. If people perform work as members of a group or community, that work is a burden which they undertake for the sake of the community. Subjectively they may experience it in a variety of ways. Sometimes they may actually enjoy the work, find it challenging or fulfilling. But objectively it is a 'burden' in the sense that it is something required of them by the community as a whole, something which they have to do,

[10] Cf. Rawls's critical discussion of the idea of justice as moral desert in *A Theory of Justice* ch. 5, section 48.
[11] My thinking about this question and the related question of 'incentives', and indeed about many other questions in this book, has been much helped by discussions with Bruce Landesman; cf. his papers 'Egalitarianism' (*Canadian Journal of Philosophy* 13, 1983) and 'The Weakness of Desert' (forthcoming).

whether they like it or not. It is therefore appropriate, from the point of view of compensation, that people should be rewarded according to the amount of work that they do. A hospital cleaner and a surgeon who have both worked an eight-hour day have both, to that extent, carried the same burden and are therefore entitled to the same compensating benefit. I have also said that the idea of compensation requires that people should get special rewards for especially demanding or dangerous work—for example, the particular hazards and demands of working as a coal-miner or a deep-sea-diver. So it might be claimed that the hospital cleaner is entitled to additional reward because the work is unpleasantly dirty, or that the surgeon is entitled to additional reward because the work involves worrying responsibilities. That may or may not be so, but from the point of view of 'compensation' it is the kind of claim which would have to be made. I think we can see from these examples that the idea of 'compensation' is an essentially egalitarian version of reward.

A second idea which has to be distinguished from the pure idea of 'desert' is that of 'incentives'. Again, this does involve a limited notion of just rewards. If, within a workplace or an economic enterprise or a profession, it is laid down in advance that those who work better will be paid more (if, for example, they are paid according to a system of piece-work), then it can intelligibly be said that if they do indeed work better, they have deserved their reward. To say that they have 'deserved' it means no more here than that they have met the specified conditions necessary for obtaining it. In this case, however, the reason for having a system of differential rewards is not that it is somehow inherently appropriate that certain people should get more, but simply that offering people special rewards may be a practical way of getting them to work better. The appeal, in other words, is not to any autonomous idea of 'merit' but to the beneficial further consequences of operating such a system. Whether a system of incentives can be accepted as just is a question I shall consider in a moment.

In contrast to the idea of 'compensation' and to that of 'incentives', the pure idea of desert is the idea that people should get special rewards simply and solely because they have done something good. It is thought to be somehow intrinsically appropriate that those who have done good deserve to receive good in return. What are we to say of this? There is one limited case in which it seems to me to be true. Those who have achieved something valuable deserve to receive such things as praise, admiration, acknowledgement, or recognition. These are indeed the intrinsically appropriate rewards for achievement. But this is because praise and other such responses are internally related to the idea of good achievements. To praise people *is* to recognize and convey to them the value of what they have done. The notion of justice may even have a role to play here. We can say that someone who has performed a good act is 'justly' praised. However, the conferring of praise is not a matter of distributive justice in the sense with which we are concerned in this chapter. Questions of distributive justice arise only when it is said that people deserve not only praise or admiration, but also other kinds of rewards such as money or other material goods. Rewards of this kind are not internally related to the recognition of achievement, and from the fact that people deserve praise it does not follow that they deserve these other goods. I cannot, in fact, see why we should accept this stronger idea of 'desert'. To return to our earlier example, the surgeon performs an extremely skilful task whereas the hospital cleaner does something which almost anyone could do, but why is the exercise of skill in itself a reason for conferring any additional benefit on the surgeon? If we are not talking about compensation, nor about incentives, I simply do not see why the conferring of such benefits should be regarded as just. The principle 'To them that have shall be given' may have the weight of biblical authority behind it, but I cannot see that there is anything more to be said for it.

It may be replied at this point that I am simply being obtuse, and am asking for some further explanation where none is needed. If someone says that there simply is something intrinsically appropriate about conferring benefits on those who have done something valuable, I do not know how to argue the matter further. We have reached deadlock. However, I should want to suggest that even if there are those who accept the pure idea of desert in its strong form, that idea can have only very limited application in a highly complex modern society with a highly differentiated division of labour. In such a society, what a person achieves will be a reflection not just of his or her efforts but of those of countless other people, or will depend upon education and training or on techniques and resources to which innumerable other people have contributed. How, for instance, can the successful businessman say that *he* has achieved this success, and that he therefore deserves all the very great material benefits it has brought him, when it derives from the co-operative endeavours of thousands of people? They include the people who work for him or with him, the people to whom he sells or from whom he buys products or materials, and all the myriads of people who help to create the social and economic conditions within which he operates. We cannot demarcate any independent area of achievement here and say 'This is his individual achievement, and he deserves to receive some special reward for it'.

I suggest, then, that the strong anti-egalitarian notion of desert is either unacceptable or at any rate inapplicable. What about the idea of 'incentives' from which I distinguished it? Can a system of incentives be just? The most influential recent account of the justification for incentives is provided by the second of Rawls's two principles of justice, which he calls 'the difference principle'. That now needs to be looked at in its own right, as another alternative principle of justice. The relevant component of the principle is that inequalities are justified if they are 'to the advantage of everyone', where this is glossed as meaning 'to the advantage of the least well off'. I want to suggest that this is another case of a principle which at one level allows certain kinds of inequalities but is itself equality-based. It is fundamentally egalitarian precisely because it takes the effect on the most disadvantaged as the test of whether inequalities are justified. The idea is that if certain kinds of social arrangements would benefit the least well off, it would be wrong to deny them that benefit. This is in keeping with what I have taken to be the tenable strand in Rawls's theory, the view of principles of equality as principles of co-operation, principles which everyone can agree to. Clearly, inequalities can be agreed to by those who are thereby made better off than others; but, they can also be agreed to by those who are rendered better off than they would otherwise have been. It is in this sense that the principle which legitimates such inequalities can be said to be egalitarian in its fundamental inspiration.[12]

Rawls himself has in mind the example of differential incentives as a form of inequality which could in practice be justified by the difference principle. However, as he acknowledges, it remains an empirical question whether this is in fact so.[13] Does a system of incentives really encourage people to work better and so leave everyone better off? No simple generalization is possible here. Obviously we can envisage cases where this would be so. However, I am also inclined to be sceptical about many applications of this idea. When it is said that people would not do work which carries special responsibilities with it, or which requires special training over a long period to acquire special skills (such as medical training), unless they had the incentive of special financial rewards, I can only say that experience suggests otherwise. There is, I think, no shortage of people who would do such work without any extra financial reward, because they recognize it to be worthwhile and because it draws on skills which they possess and which they enjoy using. It also has to be said that a system of differential rewards, if it becomes a rigidly structured hierarchy, may offer incentives to people who can get to the top but is more likely to have a

---

[12] My acceptance of Rawls's difference principle may look like a substantial weakening of my defence of equality. Thus Kai Nielsen, whose account of equality is very similar to my own in its substantial content, thinks it necessary to reject the difference principle in favour of a stronger principle of equality (see his *Equality and Liberty: A Defense of Radical Egalitarianism* (New Jersey 1985) and his 'Class and Justice' in Arthur and Shaw, *Justice and Economic Distribution*. However, there are two reasons why I do not think that my defence of equality is excessively weakened at this point: (i) although the difference principle can justify major departures from strict equality in principle, I am sceptical of its capacity to justify major inequalities in practice; (ii) whereas Rawls's first principle, which has priority over the difference principle, is a somewhat limited principle of equal liberty (cf. his list of basic liberties on p. 61), my own account would subordinate the difference principle to a strong principle of equal power. It is this emphasis on equality of power which would lead me to agree with Nielsen, and disagree with Rawls, about the necessary connection between equality and the elimination of classes. I shall return to these matters at the end of chapter 6.

[13] Rawls, *A Theory of Justice*, p. 78.

demoralizing effect on everyone else. It is likely to do so by giving them a diminished sense of personal worth, and making them disinclined to identify with the work which they do and the institution for which they do it, or to put any untoward effort or energy into that work.

It might be suggested that the kinds of incentives I have considered constitute a rather special case, and that we need to consider the more general case—the fact that most people would not work at all, would not perform the tasks required of them by the community, without the incentive of being rewarded for their efforts. Again it might be said that incentives are needed not so much to encourage people to 'get to the top', but to get people to do particularly unattractive work. At this point, however, the idea of 'incentives' coincides with that of 'compensation'. If work of one kind or another is so unattractive that no one will perform it, that will itself be an indication that greater compensation needs to be offered to balance its unpleasantness. Incentives of this kind are thus consistent with egalitarian justice; egalitarians need not deny that, in a community such as a large-scale modern economy, it is appropriate for people to be paid for their work, to be paid more if they do more work, and to be paid more if they do particularly unattractive work.

One other kind of incentive should perhaps be mentioned. It might be claimed that even though people's skills and efforts may not necessarily need to be called forth by material incentives, people will not give of their best unless their efforts are given social recognition. Therefore, the argument might go, a functioning community of any appreciable size will necessarily have to incorporate inequalities of social status, reflecting the different recognition given to different levels of achievement.

The truth in this view, I believe, is that people do indeed need recognition. Not only do they need it, but the giving of such recognition is a natural response to any human excellence. The point here is the one which I made a few paragraphs ago: praise and admiration are the naturally appropriate ways of acknowledging achievement. Egalitarianism is sometimes depicted as a recipe for monotonous mediocrity. In a society of equality, it is said, no one could ever excel at anything, since everyone would have to be held down to the same level of achievement. That, however, is a caricature of egalitarianism, a position which no advocate of equality need feel called upon to defend. There will always be those who excel, in athletic prowess or cultural achievement or intellectual ability or organizational skill. They will be admired for their excellence, looked up to, held up as models for others to emulate. Recognition of this kind is not a proper matter for distributive justice; it is simply given to those who deserve it, and to that extent no egalitarian need be opposed to inequalities of status and prestige.

The problems arise when social status becomes more than a mere matter of recognition for excellence. That regularly happens. In a profession with a hierarchical career structure, higher status will typically bring with it greater material rewards, usually in the form of higher pay. Perhaps more insidiously, inequalities of prestige may lead to inequalities of power. Someone who is looked up to may well carry a great deal of influence; that influence can easily come to inhibit criticism and independent thought on the part of others, and to a greater or lesser extent it may then come to be institutionalized as a form of power. When status carries with it power and material rewards in this way, it is clearly incompatible with the principles of equality I am defending. But I have argued that though people need the incentive of recognition, it does not follow that they need these further incentives. Therefore there is no reason here for overriding the presumption of equality.

I am, then, sceptical about the empirical claim that people need incentives in the shape of unequal rewards, and that a system of incentives would therefore be a form of justified inequality. This conclusion also provides an answer to our earlier problem about co-operation and competition. The question was whether, from a position of equal power, the members of a community might co-operatively support a competitive system allotting unequal rewards. The standard case of this would be a system of incentives, and my remarks about incentives apply also to the notion of competition. Egalitarian justice would not prevent people from seeking to emulate one another in skilled tasks and activities, and competing for praise and recognition. There is, however, no convincing reason for supposing that competition for highly unequal material rewards is a necessary feature of an efficiently-working society.[14]

I have now considered a number of alternative principles of justice. I have argued that the principle of needs, the idea of compensation, and Rawls's difference principle are all fundamentally egalitarian, introducing complexities into egalitarian justice rather than opposing it. I have suggested that the case for incentives, though it could theoretically be made in terms of Rawls's difference principle, is in practice unconvincing, at least in ways which offer any challenge to egalitarianism. The one principle which is straightforwardly anti-egalitarian is what I have called 'the pure idea of desert', but I have argued that this, when clearly distinguished from the ideas of 'compensation' and of 'incentives', and when extended beyond the central case of someone's deserving praise, seems unacceptable. I conclude that the presumption of equal benefit cannot easily be overridden by alternative principles of justice. There may be other reasons for overriding the presumption of equality, which do not appeal to principles of distribution at all. The most important claim to that effect is the one which is a central concern of this book: the suggestion that the pursuit of equality is dangerous and undesirable because it is liable to destroy people's freedom. I shall work round to the direct confrontation of that claim in chapter 7. For now I hope to have shown that the principle of equal power and a strong presumption of equal benefit make up a conception of justice which is grounded in the idea of a co-operative community.

---

[14] The sphere of sport is a good example of these points. Sporting activities are by their very nature competitive. There are bound to be winners and losers, and egalitarians need have no objection to this. A particular sport could be run very co-operatively, and this would be perfectly consistent with its competitive character. However, when international stars win huge prize money, such inequalities may undermine the co-operative aspect of the sport, which may come to be dominated by the big stars. Even so, this could perhaps in principle be justified on Rawlsian grounds; the stars bring in money which helps to fund facilities for the ordinary players or athletes at the local level. I am, however, sceptical of the claim that such vast inequalities are needed to achieve this.

## 5

# The Social Context of Equality

MY argument for equality is one which insists on locating it in a social context. In the present chapter I want to develop that idea further. I shall first look at some objections to my theory on that account. Having, I hope, rebutted these objections, I shall then consider the further implications which this has for our understanding of the nature of equality.

Principles of equality are the principles appropriate to a co-operative community. That seems to prompt the question: what if a community is *not* a co-operative community? Would that mean that the requirement of equality was not applicable? This would seem to be a very damaging implication of my account, for one would think that it is precisely where a community is not co-operative, where for example it is coercive or exploitative, that one would want to argue for equality. My account, however, appears to preclude our doing so, for I seem to be committed to saying that since the community in question is not a co-operative one, principles of equality have no place there.

There are two responses which I want to make here. One is that most actual social institutions are contradictory in this respect. They are neither purely co-operative nor purely coercive or exploitative. Take the case of a business enterprise. It may embody great inequalities; the employees may earn very poor wages, or at any rate earn a good deal less than the management or than the profits of the owners, and they may have virtually no say in the running of things. Nevertheless those who run the business are, I imagine, likely to be the first to insist that they envisage it as a joint enterprise in which all share, in which all, employers and employees, freely co-operate. Notoriously, such language is regularly heard as a response to trade union actions and disputes, and of course the same language is constantly employed at the national level: 'We're all in this together, let's all work together in a spirit of co-operation instead of being divided by sectional interests.' What I want to suggest is that if this conception of a particular social institution or of a whole society is to be taken seriously, if it is to be adopted consistently, then it requires the application of the principle of equality to the distribution of powers and benefits within the institution or the society. An enterprise which purports to be co-operative is not genuinely co-operative unless it is egalitarian.

I am not suggesting that this argument for equality is merely *ad hominem*. I am not merely saying that if people use the rhetoric of co-operation, one can throw it back at them. Of course it *is* rhetoric, often it is phoney rhetoric, but it is not *mere* rhetoric. People are enabled to use such rhetoric because there is an element of truth in it. The institutions to which it is applied may be partly coercive or exploitative, but they are not wholly so, they involve also an element of free co-operation, and that element in them constitutes the standpoint from which one can argue the need for equality.

The other kind of argument which can be mounted is that in so far as social institutions are not co-operative, they ought to be. Principles of equality are principles of co-operation, and equality is therefore desirable because co-operative social institutions are desirable. Why are they desirable? One kind of consideration which can be advanced is that people benefit from participating in co-operative activities and ways of life. Some of the benefits are obvious. One can make a better life for oneself if one shares one's energies with others, in relations of open trust which enable one to see others as allies rather than as competitors or even enemies. There are also the more intangible benefits—the benefits of widening one's interests and enlarging one's life through identifying with others and sharing their concerns, the benefits of living in harmony with one's fellows.

These are considerations which suggest that each individual gains from relations of co-operation. The same considerations could of course be formulated as utilitarian arguments aiming to show that co-operation promotes the general happiness. Through co-operation people can achieve greater levels of material prosperity, they can enjoy the advantages of living in peace and harmony and security. It is important to emphasize that this would not be a direct utilitarian argument for equality. I have previously criticized that approach. The argument I am considering now would be a two-stage argument. People benefit from relations of co-operation, and that is a reason for entering into such relations; but in doing so, they take on a commitment to treat others in certain ways—specifically, to treat them as equals. The argument is, then, an indirect argument, for equality via co-operation.

These arguments, appealing to individual and general interests, can take us a good deal of the way in providing reasons for co-operation, but they cannot, I think, take us all the way. We have to remember that the notion of co-operation which I have been invoking is co-operation in a strong sense, stronger than the mere idea of social relations in which people's skills and energies are co-ordinated to greater effect. A society based on slave labour, in which great feats of architecture or construction, such as the building of the pyramids, are achieved through the systematically organized deployment of gangs of slaves, may illustrate the benefits of co-operation in one sense; the co-ordinated strength of large numbers of people can execute tasks which individuals or small groups could never hope to perform. This, however, is not a co-operative community in the sense in which I have been using the term, contrasting it with relations of coercion or exploitation. All the more vulnerable are arguments which appeal to the interests of the individual. The gains to the individual of co-operation with others are apparent, but there are also the attractions of exploiting others, benefitting from their joint efforts but not genuinely co-operating with them.

A co-operative group or community in the strong sense is, I have said, one in which individuals freely participate and respect one another's freedom. It is as such that, in the end, it has to be defended. The fundamental reason why we should seek to promote and maintain relations of co-operation is that we ought to live and work with others in ways which respect their freedom within the common project, recognizing that they have their own needs and interests which have to be accommodated and their own ideas about how to do this. The ultimate appeal is to something like Kant's notion of 'respect for persons'—respect for them as free, autonomous beings.[1]

Again this is a two-stage argument. Respect for others as free beings does not provide a direct argument for equality. If we could live pretty much as isolated individuals, we could respect the freedom of others in a negative way, by leaving them to get on with their own lives. But as social beings, needing to associate with others and to link our efforts with theirs in common projects, our concern for the value of freedom requires that we shape our social institutions as ones in which all can participate freely, on terms which all can freely accept. Respect for persons as free beings is thus the reason for making our institutions co-operative institutions, and the principles of justice appropriate to such a co-operative group or community are then principles of equality. The relevance of all this to our earlier discussion of freedom, and to our concern with the relation between freedom and equality, should be obvious.

So much, then, for the objection that a community may not be a co-operative community. My reply is, first, that most actual communities are contradictory, partly co-operative and partly not, and that we can appeal to the co-operative aspect as the basis for criticism of the non-co-operative features; and, secondly, that in so far as a group or community is not a co-operative one, we can argue that it ought to be. But now a further and more fundamental objection may emerge. Why tie equality to membership of a group or community at all? It may be objected that such an account makes it all too easy to evade the requirements of equality. It is open to anyone, it would seem, to claim that they do not need to treat certain

---

[1] Kant's classic discussion of 'respect for persons' is in the Second Section of his *Fundamental Principles of the Metaphysics of Morals* (first published 1785). I deliberately limit myself to invoking '*something like* Kant's notion'. It would have to be detached from the metaphysics within which Kant locates it. For Kant, 'respect' is primarily respect for the moral law, and therefore derivatively respect for persons as moral agents, embodiments of the moral law. The free, rational, moral self which is the object of respect is the 'noumenal' self, contrasted with the 'phenomenal' self, the human being made up of desires and inclinations and immersed in the physical world of space and time and causality. As against Kant, I would want to base 'respect for persons' in the natural attitude of respect for human beings as 'phenomenal' beings, people with lives of their own, with their own hopes and fears, wishes and desires.

other people as equals, because they do not regard them as members of the same community. The privileged could thus say of the underprivileged: 'They are one community and we are another, we live in different worlds, and there are therefore no grounds for criticizing the inequalities between us.' In this way my account may seem to allow people to disavow their responsibilities simply by drawing the boundaries of their community in a convenient place.

Underlying this objection is the assumption that social ties and relationships are things which can be created or negated at will. This, however, is simply not the case. My earlier example, of a group of people setting up house together, is misleadingly atypical in this respect. Most human communities are not like that. They are not normally consciously created. More often a community is something into which one is born, and to which one is tied by a network of dependencies and relationships, such as family and economic ties, which are not of one's own making. Admittedly it is not always like that. There are many different kinds of communities, their membership is determined in different ways, and in some cases they are of a kind which one can consciously join (such as clubs and voluntary organizations) or which a number of people can deliberately set up (such as a communal household). Again, people can sometimes choose to change their community membership, for example by emigrating. But the general point here is that any human community has an objective existence, and its boundaries and membership cannot just be determined by arbitrary fiat. There may sometimes be difficulties in determining what those boundaries are, and in assessing the competing claims of overlapping communities; I shall say more about this in the next chapter. The fact remains, however, that these are matters to be objectively determined, and one cannot just say what one likes in order to suit one's convenience.

Consider a topical example. In present-day South Africa the doctrine of 'apartheid' is an attempt to legitimate the inequalities between blacks and whites by treating the two groups as separate communities. The black population is relegated by the white régime to artificially created 'homelands', leaving the rest of the country to be designated as belonging to the whites. The blacks who live in South Africa outside the homelands are denied South African citizenship and held to be citizens of the homelands (at the time of writing, the South African President has recently announced a decision to reverse this policy). The South African régime then defends its denial of political and social rights to its black population by claiming that they are a separate community, citizens of separate independent states.

The example may at first appear to support the objection to my own account. Here, it may be said, is a classic example of people evading the requirements of equality by refusing to apply them beyond the boundaries of their own community, and that shows how wrong it is to tie the idea of equality to that of a co-operative community. In fact, however, the example works in the other direction. The plain fact is that the black population *are* members of the South African community, and in denying this the white régime is distorting the true state of affairs. Talk of 'the black community' and 'the white community' has some application, but the fact is also that the two groups (with others) constitute a single community. A number of considerations are relevant here. Most obviously, the blacks *live in* South Africa. That does not by itself settle the matter; it is possible for people to live in a country as resident aliens. In the present case, however, the facts of residence are backed by the facts of history. This has been the country of past generations of the black population, and hence the present generation are there not as aliens but because they belong there. Their membership of the community is founded not only in the past but in the present, and most obviously in the economic life of the present. They make up the bulk of the working population, and without their co-operation the economic life of the community would collapse. I am not going to attempt here a systematic account of the criteria for membership of a community, as they apply to this example or to any other. I want merely to insist that there *are* objective criteria, and that one cannot just define the boundaries of a community in whatever way one wishes.

One might also seek to evade the requirements of equality not by excluding others from the community, but by excluding oneself. Would this be possible, according to my account? Here the case is slightly different, but the essential point still stands. One can, in principle, opt out of a community and refuse to be a member of it, and according to my account this would indeed have the implication that one then had no reason to regard one's relation to the other members as one of equality. However, the opting out would have to be a real opting out, and I suspect that the kinds of example which readily come to mind and appear damaging to my position would *not* be examples of real opting out. Take the case of someone who amasses a fortune and who then objects to paying high taxes and attempts to evade them, saying that he has no wish to be part of this system of redistribution; he has made his own money and he asks only to be left alone to look after himself and leave others to do the same. This may look like 'opting out of the community' but it is in fact only a truncated version of opting out, a rejection only of those parts which it suits him to reject. He has made his fortune through his membership of the community, and this in itself would leave him with obligations even if he were physically to remove himself; all the more would those obligations continue if he were to remain and enjoy the benefits of membership while proclaiming himself a non-member. So, though opting out is possible, one does not cease to be a member of a community just by saying so. Again the point is that membership of a community is determined by objective facts about the relations between people.

Confining equality to specific communities, then, does not provide a licence for evading its demands. Nevertheless, this may still be felt to be too limited a view of equality. Should it not extend beyond the boundaries of all particular communities? In the modern world the dominant form of community is the nation-state, and in practice much of the political debate about equality is concerned with the proper ordering of the nation-state. But the ideal of equality has also often been associated with universalistic ethical ideas, with assertions of the unity of mankind and the claim that 'all men are equal'. Does this not take us beyond any organized community? What about the problems of world hunger, for example? Should principles of equality not govern the relations between the mainly prosperous inhabitants of Europe and North America and the desperately poor populations of most of Africa, Asia, and Latin America?

Undoubtedly most people would say that those of us who are relatively prosperous by global standards ought, morally, to do something to ease the appalling burden of poverty in the Third World. Some such response would be the expression of a natural human sympathy. But to say this is to employ the moral language of 'compassion', of 'charity', and so on; it is not yet to employ the language of 'equality'. Is the idea of equality an appropriate one here? I am not sure of the answer, but I want to say that it is appropriate just in so far as we can appropriately talk of a 'world community'.

The point may be clearer if we compare a hypothetical case. Suppose that we discovered a distant planet to be inhabited by beings who could, to all intents and purposes, be called 'human'. Suppose that we could communicate with them, and discovered that they thought and reasoned as we do, and suppose that they were sufficiently like us biologically to have much the same physical needs. Suppose that their needs were grossly undersatisfied, that they were ravaged by disease and starvation and lived lives of much greater suffering than us. It seems to me that it would be implausible to regard the differences between our situation and theirs as unjust inequalities. As we come to find out more about their situation, we might be moved by their suffering and feel that we ought to do something to help them. But so long as we and they remained, simply and literally, the inhabitants of different worlds, I do not think that our relations with them would appropriately be judged by reference to principles of equality, and it could not plausibly be said that we were treating them unjustly by not pooling our resources and sharing equally with them.[2]

Now the relations between rich and poor in our world are

[2] Along similar lines I would argue that 'equality' is not an appropriate ethical concept to apply to our relations with animals. Cf. Lesley Pickering Francis and Richard Norman, 'Some Animals Are More Equal Than Others' (*Philosophy*, vol. 53, 1978). The most eloquent advocate of the opposing view is Peter Singer, and this is entirely consistent with his general account of equality which I have mentioned in chapter 4. See for example his *Animal Liberation* (New York 1975) and *Practical Ethics* (Cambridge 1979) ch. 3.

not like that. At one time they may have been—three or four centuries ago, when the European nations were making their first contacts with other societies. But the relations between different societies are now much closer. The growth of trade, of a network of dependencies between industrialized and non-industrialized societies, of investment in other countries by individuals, firms, and now by multi-national corporations, all of this has created what can properly be called a single world economy. In its wake, political institutions on a world scale are gradually and painfully emerging. It becomes appropriate to talk of the exploitation of some societies by others within the world economy. To that extent we are invoking the ideal of equality as an appropriate one to govern the relations between those societies, and whether we can treat it as a practically feasible ideal depends on whether we can envisage a world political community eventually taking shape. I do not, then, think that there is a clear and simple answer to the question 'Do principles of equality apply on a larger scale than that of the nation-state?' and I do not think that there is a clear and simple answer to the question 'Is there a world community?' I do, however, think that the two claims stand or fall together.

I wish, then, to stick to the claim that the ideal of equality is not a general moral ideal applicable to all human actions and interactions, but an ideal specifically applicable to the distribution of power and of benefits within a co-operative community. Discussion of the objections, however, has made it clear that we need to look more closely at the different kinds of communities with which we are concerned. If there are problems with the idea of a co-operative community larger than the nation state, there can be no doubt about the existence of co-operative communities on a smaller scale. There is a vast range of them—towns and cities and other local communities; economic associations from nationalized industries and large corporations to small factories and workshops; other kinds of workplaces concerned with the provision of public services, such as schools and universities and hospitals; and voluntary associations and clubs of all kinds. In all of these, there arises the problem of how to allot roles and responsibilities, how to distribute rewards, how to share out the goods which the association creates. In all of them, therefore, principles of equality have their place, as the requirement that this distribution should be consonant with the character of the association as a co-operative enterprise.

The existence of this range of co-operative institutions, small and large, and the fact that they overlap with one another, now creates further difficulties. These various institutions do not exist in self-contained isolation; the smaller ones are normally located within larger communities, members of a larger community will also be members of a number of different smaller communities, and consequently the requirements of equality in one institution will sometimes conflict with the requirements of equality in another. To take one example, experience suggests that decentralized workers' control of economic units tends to produce a relatively egalitarian wage structure within the local economic unit, but also tends to produce greater wage inequalities over the society as a whole compared with a more centralized system, since the autonomy allowed to individual economic units enables some of them to be more successful than others. From the point of view of equality, is the decentralized or the centralized structure to be preferred? It might be thought that the requirements of equality on a larger scale should take precedence over those of equality on a smaller scale, for it might seem that this would make for greater equality overall. In practice, however, the choice may inescapably be between different kinds of equalities and inequalities which balance one another out, so that no one option can straightforwardly be seen as a choice for 'greater equality overall'. In the case of our example, the decentralized structure may make for greater equality as between manual workers and managerial staff, and between skilled and unskilled workers, but at a cost of greater imbalances between the prosperous and less prosperous parts of the country, whereas the centralized structure may be able to correct the regional imbalances but produce greater wage differentials. Neither option presents itself straightforwardly as a choice for greater equality. The picture is further complicated by the fact that other considerations may also be relevant to the choice between the conflicting requirements of different communities. In our example, the decentralized structure might be preferred on the grounds that it is more efficient, or that it encourages greater democratic participation (which in turn is linked with the desirability of other kinds of equality). There is, then, no simple answer to the question 'What do we do when the requirements of equality in one community conflict with the requirements of equality in another overlapping community?' I simply want to say that this difficulty is no objection to my account of equality. The difficulty is one which does indeed occur, such tensions do indeed arise in our practical thinking about equality, and a theory which failed to offer any account of them would be the poorer.

Although there is a vast range of communities whose distributive arrangements are properly matters for equality, there are also aspects of human life which lie outside the domain of equality. The obvious example is that of 'personal relations'—the sphere of love, friendship, and sexual relations. Critics of equality have sometimes caricatured it as requiring the elimination of exclusive emotions and sexual preferences: egalitarians who love one person in a special way are being unfair to all the other people amongst whom they should have distributed their love. Now that is indeed a caricature of egalitarianism, but it is not easy to say why it is a caricature unless we recognize that equality is an ideal specific to the life of a co-operative community, not a totally general moral idea. Love and friendship and sexual intimacy are not candidates for equal distribution, because they are not allotted by communal arrangements. Plato's prescriptions for the regulation of sexual relationships in the *Republic* are the exception which proves the rule. Plato is not a strict egalitarian in these matters; he thinks that, within the Guardian class, the best men should mate with the best women, and the inferior with the inferior. Nevertheless, it is clear that he thinks that people's sexual favours should be 'distributed' pretty widely—and 'distributed' is precisely the right word here, for he sees this as a matter for communal regulation. Conversely we can say that principles of equality are not appropriate principles to govern the forming of sexual ties and relationships, or any other intimate relationships, because these are not the proper subject for communal decision-making and regulation.

Even here, however, the matter is not as simple as that. Characteristically, lovers are not just lovers, they often marry or set up house together. What begins as a close sexual relationship then becomes a partnership encompassing many other aspects of people's lives together. Sexual intimacy inescapably evolves into sexual politics, and familiar dilemmas arise about the respective roles of sexual partners—how are tasks of house-keeping and child-rearing to be allotted, should both partners work outside the home, will one partner's career take precedence over the other's? Clearly principles of equality will be appropriate here, but there will also be an inevitable tension between the relative formalization of roles which it requires and the spontaneity of a close emotional relationship. No theory of equality can conjure away that tension, but it will at any rate be a strength, not a weakness, in a theory that it recognizes the existence of these complexities.

So far, then, I have tried to show that the difficulties which are raised by linking the idea of equality to that of a co-operative community are not grounds for criticism but are, on the contrary, the kinds of difficulty which we should expect to see reflected in any adequate notion of equality. I want now to start building up a fuller account of the content of equality. I suggested at the beginning of the previous chapter that we could not decide exactly what we were arguing for, when arguing for equality, until we had decided which arguments were valid. I hope that this reversal of the natural sequence can now be seen to be vindicated. In developing my arguments in defence of equality, I have also begun to develop an account of what a defensible version of equality would consist in. It may be helpful at this point if we compare that emerging picture with some other current conceptions of equality. I begin with another caricature. It has sometimes been suggested that egalitarians are committed to an ideal of making everyone alike. A society of equals would, it is said, be a society in which all individuality was lost, and in which everyone was dragooned into a monotonous uniformity. That account is a nonsense. No egalitarian has ever maintained it, and my own account of equality is far removed from it. The principle of equality in the distribution of benefits and burdens, which I have presented as the second of my two principles in the previous chapter, does not mean that everyone has to receive the *same* benefits, or, for that matter, to shoulder the same burdens. What is required is that, as far as possible, everyone should benefit equally overall. Different people may choose different kinds of benefit. There will be other differences which are not matters of choice but are inescapable: some people will have to carry special burdens and will have to be compensated with special benefits; some people may enjoy benefits which not everyone can share, and others will therefore obtain alternative benefits in their stead. There is, in short, ample room for diversity within the egalitarian ideal.

As an improvement on that caricature, we could consider the version of equality which has sometimes been formulated as 'equal well-being'.[3] This looks more like my own idea of 'equal benefit'; different people, I have said, will enjoy different benefits and carry different burdens, but everybody should enjoy as good a life overall as everyone else. As it stands, however, the phrase 'equal well-being' still looks rather general, and we may wonder whether it does sufficient justice to the great differences between individuals. Not only is it the case that different people have different tastes and talents and will therefore choose to fulfil themselves in different ways. It also seems sadly and inescapably to be the case that some people have a talent for making the most of their lives, whilst others have a talent for making a mess of their lives. How on earth can we bring them all to a common level of well-being? We seem to be back with the attempt to force people's diverse characters and temperaments into a uniform mould.

To escape that implication, many writers have favoured a more limited notion of equality—the ideal of 'equality of opportunity'.[4] We cannot, they say, guarantee everyone an

---

[3] For a detailed and persuasive exploration of the idea of 'equal well-being', see Bruce Landesman, 'Egalitarianism'.

[4] An example is John Plamenatz: 'Equality of Opportunity', in Lyman Bigson *et al* (eds.) *Aspects of Human Equality*, (New York 1957); reprinted in James Rachels

equally worthwhile life, but we can give everyone an equal opportunity, and it is then up to individuals to make what they will of the opportunities. That looks like a judiciously modest narrowing of the concept, but to assess it properly we need to know more. We need to know what kinds of thing are to count as 'opportunities', and what they are opportunities *for*. In practice, the concept tends to be employed against the background of a competitive struggle for unequal rewards. It is invoked particularly in discussions of educational policy, where it is suggested that the educational system should sort children according to their abilities, using competitive examinations to distinguish the successes and the failures, but that every child should have the same chance to compete. As in a race, it is said, not everyone can win, but at least we can make sure that everyone starts at the same place and no one has an unfair advantage or disadvantage. This is taken to mean that state schooling should be made available to all children regardless of class, sex, race, or parental wealth, and that the same standards should be applied to all of them to test their abilities and achievements. This vision of 'equality of opportunity' in the sphere of education is sometimes extended also to society as a whole. It is suggested that the same standards of 'fair competition' should be applied also to competition for jobs, promotions, and the greater or lesser rewards which go with them; there too no one should be unfairly advantaged or disadvantaged by his or her social origins. Educational achievements will, in fact, themselves be one of the main ways of determining that people get the jobs and the rewards for which they are properly qualified. So there emerges a picture of the whole of society as one vast competition, a race in which, at birth, everyone is on the same starting line, but in which, thereafter, some fall further and further behind as others forge ahead.

It is clear that this vision cannot convincingly be called an

and Frank A. Tillman (eds.) *Philosophical Issues* (New York 1972). Enthusiastic political advocacy of equal opportunity is to be found in C. A. R. Crosland *The Future of Socialism* (London 1956, revised edn. 1963), but Crosland also says quite explicitly that 'equal opportunity is not enough'. Equality of opportunity is discussed and given qualified endorsement in Bernard Williams, 'The Idea of Equality'. It is forcefully criticized in Singer, *Practical Ethics* ch. 3, and in Kai Nielsen, *Equality and Liberty* chs. 7–8; Nielsen also provides useful further references.

egalitarian one. It is, on the contrary, a vision of a hierarchical society—a ladder of success on which all have their place, high or low, and the organization of the society is devoted to ensuring that each person finds his or her proper place. This may be an attractive ideal for some, but it will certainly not be attractive to those who are looking for an acceptable notion of *equality*.[5] Does this mean that we should abandon forthwith the idea of 'equality of opportunity'? Not necessarily, for, as I indicated, what we understand by the phrase will depend on what we mean by 'opportunity'. The interpretation which we have just considered takes 'equal opportunity' to mean 'equal opportunity to compete for limited prizes'—in other words, 'equal opportunity to be unequal'. Suppose now that we were to interpret it more widely, to mean 'equal opportunity for everyone to enjoy a good life'. This suggests a very different picture from the one which we have just considered, for the competitive society which we described was certainly not one in which everyone has an equal opportunity to enjoy a good life; on the contrary, it was one in which some people enjoy much greater rewards than others. Our new interpretation, on the other hand, looks genuinely egalitarian. It seems to express the idea of equal well-being when qualified in the way that it needs to be—the idea that, though we cannot guarantee to everyone an equally good life, we can organize our social arrangements so that they do not give anyone less chance of a good life than anyone else, and the differences in the quality of people's lives are simply the outcome of their particular choices and temperaments.

More still needs to be said, however. Our formulation now depends on a distinction between the socially-organized determinants of people's well-being and those more particular determinants which are not socially regulated. Can that distinction be firmly drawn? It seems, on the contrary, to be a line which can be varied at will. There is not, in principle, any final distinction to be made between those aspects of people's

---

[5] I allowed in chapter 4 that the notion of a co-operative community is in principle not incompatible with elements of competition. Nevertheless they would have to be embedded within a fundamentally egalitarian system, and that is something quite different from a purely competitive system.

lives which can, and those which cannot, be determined by social arrangements. With advances in genetic engineering we could, perhaps, bring it about that the effects of temperamental differences between people were minimized, everyone had the same happy disposition and no one was more liable than anyone else to depression or dejection; we could bring the rearing of children under very strict social supervision so as to ensure that no child had a more favourable upbringing than any other. These are possibilities. They are not now, but they could become, socially-organized determinants of people's well-being. Where we draw the line is therefore, inescapably, a matter for decision. We have to decide whether we *want* genetic engineering, we have to decide whether we *want* state-supervised child-rearing, and in deciding that, we shall be deciding where the principle of equality is to be applied and where it is not. Other values will therefore have to come into play. We might decide, for instance, that though people's chances of enjoying a good life could be made more equal by the means we have mentioned, they would constitute an intolerable invasion of privacy (in the legitimate sense identified at the end of chapter 3), or would diminish the rich variety of human life. We would then be deciding that, for the sake of other values, we did not wish principles of equality to be applied to these aspects of people's lives.

There is one other way in which we might try to demarcate the sphere of the socially organized determinants of human well-being. We might try to distinguish between the structure of a community and what goes on within the structure. By 'structure' we would mean the relatively formalized rules governing the relationships between the different groups or different roles within the community, constituting the framework within which the activities of the community take place. Thus the structure of a feudal society would be the set of rules specifying the economic and political obligations which the various feudal estates owed to one another; the structure of the patriarchal family would be the conventions whereby the husband exercised authority and economic power and the wife's role was one of obedience and the performance of domestic tasks. These would be examples of structures of inequality, and we could think of equality as likewise a feature of the basic structure of a community, leaving unregulated the activities of people within that structure.

Now again that distinction does not solve anything, for it still leaves open the question how much of the activities of a community should be incorporated within its formal structure and how much should be left unstructured. Our imagined society based on 'genetic engineering' would be one in which breeding arrangements guided by a scientific knowledge of genetics had become part of the structure of society. Thus the distinction between the structure and what goes on within the structure still leaves it a matter for decision where the line is to be drawn. For all that, the notion of 'structure' is useful as indicating an important application of the principle of equality. But it would be wrong to confine equality simply to the structure of a community. A particular community could have a formal structure which appeared very egalitarian, and yet be highly unequal in its actual workings. Take the case of racial inequalities. These may be part of the institutionalized structure of a society, with formal rules excluding blacks from positions of power and influence and confining them to inferior positions (contemporary South Africa is the obvious example). But racial inequalities may also be primarily a matter of habitual attitudes and prejudices rather than institutionalized rules. It may be the case that blacks are not formally barred from exercising political power or holding certain kinds of jobs, but are effectively prevented from doing so by the attitudes of a white majority. The latter kind of inequality would seem to be just as important as the former.

The discussion so far may seem rather inconclusive. I have said that principles of equality are properly applied to those distributions of powers and of benefits which are the concern of a co-operative community. There appears to be no simple way of demarcating the range of such distributions. Nevertheless, there are some things that we have been able to say, even if they are mainly negative. We have seen that the assimilation of 'equality' to 'uniformity' is quite untenable, and is a caricature of the idea which egalitarians have wanted to defend. More acceptable as a description of at least part of the egalitarian ideal is the phrase 'equality of well-being', but this as it stands is too wide and needs to be qualified. On the other hand the phrase 'equality of opportunity' as it is frequently understood is too narrow, sometimes so narrow that it ceases to be an egalitarian notion at all. It can, however, be given a more acceptable interpretation, and if taken to mean something like 'equality of opportunity to enjoy a good life' it comes closer to the notion we want. But we still have to say what those 'opportunities' are which it is the business of a co-operative community to distribute. They include, but are not confined to, those features of a community or society which constitute its structure. If we are looking for a single phrase to sum up the idea which we are working towards, I would suggest William Morris's phrase 'equality of condition', where the word 'condition' is used in its traditional sense to mean a person's social position (as in the Prayer-book's reference to 'all sorts and conditions of men').[6]

I do not think we can advance any further in defining our notion of equality at this level of generality. What we can do is to specify more precisely those structural features and those 'opportunities for well-being' which are properly matters for social distribution. We should first return to the distinction which I made in the previous chapter between 'equality of power' and 'equality of benefits', and should emphasize again the primary importance of power. Within the category of 'benefits' we can usefully introduce a broad distinction between 'material benefits' and 'cultural benefits' (including, in particular, educational opportunities). We thus arrive at a threefold classification matching the way in which, in Chapter 3, I classified the conditions of freedom. In the next chapter I shall spell out in more detail the kinds of social and distributive arrangements which would make for equality of power, equality of material goods, and equality of cultural and educational opportunities.

[6] See his lectures 'How We Live and How We Might Live' (delivered in 1884), 'The Society of the Future' (delivered in 1887), and 'Communism' (delivered in 1893). These are included in *The Political Writings of William Morris*, ed. A. L. Morton (London 1973). The phrase 'equality of condition' is explicitly introduced on pp. 158, 201, 210, and 238. The same phrase is also employed by Kai Nielsen, who defines his use of it on pp. 283–4 of his *Equality and Liberty*.

# 6

## Components of Equality

When we are thinking about power in a whole society such as the modern nation-state, we are likely to think first of political power in the orthodox sense—the power exercised by the legitimate government. But if political power is something exercised by governments, how can it also be shared equally? The extension of power from governments to the ordinary members of a society is the hallmark of a democratic political system, but if it is to come anywhere near equality of power it requires a form of democracy much more radical than anything we know at present. In the system of parliamentary democracy with which we are familiar, everyone (above a certain age) has a vote, and the power constituted by that right to vote is therefore equally shared. It is clear, however, that it is a very limited power, miniscule when compared with the power held by political leaders. If we were to aim at greater equality of power, and therefore at a more radical democracy, what form could this plausibly take? I shall try to say something more about this in chapter 8, but for the moment, in order to make the idea even initially plausible, I need to point out that it does not necessarily mean that every political decision has to be a collective decision of the whole society—government by referendum, as it were. The use of referenda might indeed feature more prominently in a radical democracy, but it is also important to recognize that equality of power is not incompatible with the delegation of responsibilities to elected delegates. If I choose someone to represent me (and we can think here of examples outside the political sphere—employing a solicitor, say, or an accountant) I do not necessarily hand over all my power to that person. How much power the representative has, and how much power I retain, will depend on how answerable the representative is to me. At one extreme, I might give him or her a free hand; at the other extreme, I might require my representative to refer every decision back to me for approval; and there is a range of possibilities between the two extremes. The general point is, then, that equality of power is compatible with the delegation of responsibilities to elected representatives but, as compared with present political practices, it requires a shift in the balance of power between electors and elected. It requires that political representatives should be more answerable to those whom they represent, so that genuine power lies with the latter. Understood in this way, equality of power may be difficult to achieve, but it is at any rate a plausible ideal at which to aim, even if we can only approximate to it.

If we are to take that ideal seriously, however, we also have to recognize that a great deal of power in society is located outside the formal political system. In particular, property is power. In part this is simply true by definition. To own a thing is to have certain rights of control over that thing, certain powers to decide what is to be done with that thing. The importance of this, however, goes beyond the mere definitional truth, for particular kinds of ownership carry other powers with them. The ownership of the means of production, of a firm or a factory or whatever, gives the owners power also over other people, power to hire and fire workers, power to decide the conditions of their work, and so on. The exercise of this power may have a drastic effect on other people's lives, as when the owners of an economic enterprise decide to close it down or to reduce the size of the work-force. Though nominally economic power it is also equally a form of political power, giving to those who wield it the ability to influence profoundly the character and the policies of their society. To take just one classic example, the owners of firms in the armaments industry use their power in order to influence government decisions in the area of defence and disarmament.

Equality of power, then, will involve the democratization not only of political power in the narrow sense, but also of the power which goes with economic ownership. This is one of the main reasons why egalitarians have, at least in the modern world, argued for the common ownership of the means of production. Moreover, if it is to make for equality of power, this will have to be not just nominal common ownership, the kind of 'nationalization' which nominally transfers the ownership of an industry to the society as a whole, through its representatives in parliament, but leaves the internal power structure of the industry virtually unchanged. It will have to involve the radically democratic sharing of effective control. Again, as with political power, there are large questions as to just what this could mean in practice. In particular there is the basic question of who should exercise democratic control: the producers (those who work in the industry or institution) or the consumers (those who make use of the goods or services which it provides) or some combination of the two. But, as before, the important general point to be made is that this radical democracy does not rule out the differentiation of functions. In any economic enterprise innumerable day-to-day decisions have to be made by those who are qualified to make them, by skilled managers and technical experts. 'Equality of power' means not that these decisions must instead be made by mass meetings of workers, but that those who make them must be effectively answerable to the wider democratic body.

The power relations created by economic ownership, when extended over a whole society, make up the contours of relations between classes. There is a fundamental division between the class of those who do, and the class of those who do not, enjoy the power which comes from ownership of the means of production. Consequently the central component of a thorough-going egalitarian politics has been the demand for the abolition of classes. Some Marxist writing has, indeed, seemed to suggest that this is the only coherent content of the idea of equality. Engels, for example, writes: '. . . the real content of the proletarian demand for equality is the demand for the *abolition of classes*. Any demand for equality which goes beyond that, of necessity passes into absurdity.'[1] That is too simple. As I have mentioned previously, the important social inequalities are not just inequalities between classes but also (as Engels himself recognizes full well in other places) inequalities between races and between the sexes, and these, though they may be causally connected with, are not

[1] Engels, *Anti-Dühring*, p. 128.

reducible to, class inequalities. Nevertheless, the idea of a classless society is clearly central to the egalitarian vision. And again it has to be stressed that this does not mean the abolition of all distinctions between different social functions. It means that the many different roles in any society counterbalance one another so that power is shared equally amongst them all; there is no limited set of roles whose occupants constitute a class enjoying a monopoly of effective power.

MATERIAL GOODS

Many critics of egalitarianism, and not a few of its defenders, have assumed that the main emphasis of an egalitarian politics must be on the equal distribution of material goods. That is, in my view, a misplaced emphasis. I take equality of power to be more fundamental than equality of wealth. In part this is because the distribution of power is more central to the character of a community than the distribution of wealth. A community in which power was equally shared, and which decided freely and democratically that some of its members should receive greater material rewards than others, would seem to me to be more egalitarian in spirit, more genuinely co-operative, than a community in which a ruling élite distributed material goods equally to everyone including themselves. On this point I can invoke the authority of Plato as an avowed anti-egalitarian. The ideal society which he describes in *The Republic* is one in which there is considerable equality of wealth. The rulers possess no personal wealth, they must share in common those limited material goods which they are allowed, and it is their task to ensure that in the society as a whole there are no extremes of wealth and poverty. They do, however, possess a total monopoly of political power, and Plato, therefore, has no doubt that the conception of justice embodied in such a society is totally at odds with the ideal of equality. His model of an egalitarian society is the Athenian city-state of his own day, in which power is shared by all the citizens, and he is bitterly critical of the way in which it has been corrupted by its surrender to equality.[2]

---

[2] The rulers' lack of private wealth is discussed in *The Republic* III, 416D–417B, and the need to avoid extremes of wealth and poverty is urged in IV, 421D–422A.

The second reason for taking equality of power to be more basic than equality of wealth is that it is causally more fundamental. Inequalities of wealth tend to be caused by inequalities of power rather than vice versa. If certain groups in society are materially a great deal better off than others, this is likely to be because they exercise the kind of power which enables them to acquire such goods for themselves. As I have just been noting, economic power itself resides largely in the ownership of certain kinds of material goods—the means of production; but these are to be contrasted with goods for consumption, and it is primarily the latter that are referred to in the phrase 'equality of wealth'.

The causal priority of economic power is emphasized especially by the Marxist tradition. So impressed is Marx with the way in which the power derived from ownership of the means of production determines the distribution of wealth in a society, that he almost seems to suggest that principles of distribution are otiose. In his *Critique of the Gotha Programme* he says:

Any distribution whatever of the means of consumption is only a consequence of the distribution of the conditions of production themselves. The latter distribution, however, is a feature of the mode of production itself. The capitalist mode of production, for example, rests on the fact that the material conditions of production are in the hands of non-workers in the form of property in capital and land, while the masses are only owners of the personal conditions of production, of labour-power. If the elements of production are so distributed, then the present-day distribution of the means of consumption results automatically. If the material conditions of production are the co-operative property of the workers themselves, then there likewise results a distribution of the means of consumption different from the present one.[3]

There is substantial truth in this. The products of human labour do not simply lie around waiting to be distributed.

The attack on equality (which is formulated also as a criticism of liberty) is to be found especially in the account of democracy in VIII, 557A–558C and 562B–563D. Democracy is described as 'dispensing equality indiscriminately to equals and unequals' (558C).

[3] *Karl Marx: Selected Writings* ed. McLellan, pp. 569–70. Subsequent references in this chapter are to the same collection.

They are produced within a particular network of economic relations, and those relations automatically assign to particular people rights of ownership over the products of labour. If I make furniture in my own back yard, using materials which I have bought for myself, the furniture I make belongs to me. If I make furniture in a factory in which I am employed, it belongs to the owner of the factory.

Nevertheless, Marx's assertion is an over-statement. There is not just one precise distribution of the means of consumption which results automatically from a particular mode of production. The latter may place severe restraints on the former, but there is still some room for manœuvre. In a capitalist economy there are differing views about how far wealth should be redistributed by means of taxation and welfare services. In a state-controlled economy there are conflicting demands on state expenditure, and there are decisions to be made about the fixing of income levels; and similar questions would arise in a communally controlled economy. It is therefore not otiose to assert, in answer to these questions, that a rational distribution of wealth would be an equal distribution.

But what does this mean? We can quickly dismiss the caricatures, such as that everyone is to have the same amount of each particular item ('Everyone is entitled to a pint of milk every day, 2 pounds of meat each week, 6 books a year.') Only slightly less of a caricature is the suggestion that economic equality means simply and solely that everyone is paid exactly the same wages, whatever their needs and however much work they do. But once we get beyond the caricatures it is by no means obvious what a more complex version of economic equality would amount to. As a convenient way of trying to throw some light on the problem, I want to examine further the passage from Marx's *Critique of the Gotha Programme*. Despite its general tone of scepticism about the usefulness of the concept of equality, it is a passage which has had a considerable influence on egalitarian thinking, and especially on socialist ideas of equality. The 'Gotha Programme' was drawn up in 1875 as a basis on which to unite the two wings of the German socialist movement, and Marx's negative tone is largely a symptom of his hostility towards the wing consisting of the followers of his rival, Lassalle. Marx criticizes the over-simple use of notions such as 'fair distribution' and 'equal right to the proceeds of labour', which he regards as examples of Lassallean influence. The more complex account which he offers in their place can, I think, be read as the application of the idea that everyone should benefit equally overall from their participation in a co-operative community. However, he does not present it as such, and sometimes seems to suggest that the complexities cast doubt on the very idea of equality.

The offending Lassallean phrases in the Gotha programme are the demand for 'a fair distribution of the proceeds of labour' and the statement that 'the proceeds of labour belong undiminished with equal right to all members of society'. Marx first points out that from the total social product must be deducted a portion for re-investment, to replace the means of production which have been used up, to expand production, and to insure against accidents, natural calamities etc. This does not, I think, present any problem for the concept of equality, for of course the demand for an equal distribution applies only to those proceeds of labour which are not reinvested and are available for distribution as means of consumption. It is simply a rather pedantic comment on the phrase 'undiminished proceeds of labour'. Marx says that the amounts to be deducted 'are in no way calculable by equity', but I do not think anyone has ever suggested that they are.

More seriously, Marx then says that further deductions would have to be made for 'the general costs of administration', for 'the common satisfaction of needs, such as schools, health services, etc.', and for 'funds for those unable to work, etc.'. What we are talking about here is the collective provision of welfare services—what we know today as 'the welfare state'. Marx notes that the resources needed for welfare services are a deduction from 'that part of the means of consumption which is divided among the individual producers of the co-operative society', but adds that 'what the producer is deprived of in his capacity as a private individual benefits him directly or indirectly in his capacity as a member of society'. What he fails to add, but could have added, is that the communal provision of such services is itself an application

of the principle of equality. Another great socialist writer,
R. H. Tawney, who is a less hesitant champion of equality
than Marx, sees the communal provision of welfare services
as the very lynchpin of a 'strategy of equality'. In his book
*Equality* (first published in 1931 and a classic of the British
labour movement) he suggests that the critics of equality,
instead of 'belabouring a phantom', should 'examine the
methods by which some inequalities, at least, have already
been diminished'.

The form which such methods have most commonly assumed is a
matter of experience. It is not the division of the nation's income
into eleven million fragments, to be distributed, without further
ado, like cake at a school treat, among its eleven million families. It
is, on the contrary, the pooling of its surplus resources by means of
taxation, and the use of the funds thus obtained to make accessible
to all, irrespective of their income, occupation, or social position,
the conditions of civilization which, in the absence of such
measures, can be enjoyed only by the rich.[4]

The equality to be achieved by these methods is not a crude
equality. It would be absurd to propose that everyone should
receive the same provision for sickness or old age or
unemployment; not everyone is unemployed or old or sick,
and those who need health care and other such services need
them in different ways and in different degrees. The
governing principle in this whole area is 'To each according
to his need', and as I have argued previously, this is itself an
egalitarian principle. It amounts to the stipulation that
everyone should benefit equally from their participation in a
co-operative community, that the most important benefit to
be gained is the satisfaction of one's basic needs, and that if
some people have special needs, special provision should be
made for them so as to bring them as close as possible to the
general standard of well-being enjoyed by their fellows.
    Turning to that part of the social product which remains to
be distributed amongst people as individuals, Marx notes
that one cannot feasibly propose a simple equality even here.
Rather, each individual will be remunerated, not indeed with

[4] R. H. Tawney, *Equality*, 4th edn. with a new Introduction by Richard M.
Titmuss (London 1964), ch. 4 (i), p. 122.

money as we know it, but with a 'certificate of labour', in proportion to the amount of work which he or she has contributed; and with this he or she will be able to draw from the social stock of means of consumption. Marx comments:

Hence, *equal right* here is still in principle—*bourgeois right* . . . The right of the producers is *proportioned* to the labour they supply; the equality consists in the fact that measurement is made with an *equal standard*, labour. But one man is superior to another physically or mentally, and so supplies more labour in the same time, or can labour for a longer time; and labour, to serve as a measure, must be defined by its duration or intensity, otherwise it ceases to be a standard of measurement. This *equal* right is an unequal right for unequal labour. It recognises no class differences, because everyone is only a worker like everyone else; but it tacitly recognises unequal individual endowment and thus productive capacity as natural privileges. *It is, therefore, a right of inequality, in its content, like every right.* (pp. 568–9)

For all his flourishing of the dialectical transformation of equality into inequality, the only 'inequality' which Marx actually seems to envisage here is that rewards would be proportional to the *amount* of work which people contribute; he is not, I think, suggesting that there would also have to be special rewards for the special skills which people might happen to possess. But then it is not clear why that so-called 'inequality' which he thinks necessary creates any problem for the idea of equality. It is simply a natural and proper consequence of the principle requiring the equal distribution of benefits and burdens, a principle which implies that if people have to carry greater burdens they are to be compensated with greater benefits. Burdens are then taken to be cancelled out by benefits, and the resultant equality is equality of *overall* benefit. In applying this principle one would reckon the amount of work which people contribute as part of the burden which they carry. Of course work could be made a good deal less burdensome than it has been in the past or is now, and Marx's vision of the future stresses this. For purposes of social distribution, however, work which is done at regular hours in a pre-ordained way, as distinct from work which is done because one happens to feel like doing it, must count as a 'burden' for which one must be compensated with proportionate benefits. The 'unequal right' which Marx points to, then, is simply the superficial aspect of a more fundamental equality.

Marx might also have mentioned, but does not, that there are other burdens which could be compensated for, besides the amount of labour. Some work, such as mining or deep-sea diving, is particularly dangerous; some is particularly unpleasant, such as that of the refuse collector or sewerage worker; and the principle of equality can perfectly well be taken to require that such disadvantages be balanced with greater remuneration. Here too the superficial inequalities would be consequences of a basic equality.

There is one further problem which Marx raises for the idea of 'equal right to the proceeds of labour'. He says:

Further, one worker is married, another not; one has more children than another, and so on and so forth. Thus, with an equal performance of labour, and hence an equal share in the social consumption fund, one will in fact receive more than another, and so on. To avoid all these defects, right instead of being equal would have to be unequal. (p. 569)

It is not entirely clear why Marx sees a problem in the fact that a worker may be married. Presumably his point is that if two people A and B both do the same amount of work for the same remuneration, and A is married whereas B is not, what A earns will have to be shared among two people and A will therefore benefit only half as much as B from the same amount of work. But of course there is no reason why marriage partners should not both work. And if they choose not to do so, if they decide that they will both live on the earnings of one of them, this is perfectly compatible with the principle of equality as I have been presenting it, involving as it does the notion of benefits as compensation for the burdens of work and thus implying that one may choose to forego both the burdens and the compensating benefits. (Bear in mind that we are assuming that the portion of the social product which is distributed in the form of welfare services is made available to everyone, whether or not they work.)

My response on this point may seem rather bland. Lurking below the surface, of course, are problems about what counts as 'work'. What if the marriage partners decide that one of them should stay at home and concentrate on the tasks of child care? Are they both 'working'? I see no reason in principle why a consistent egalitarian policy should not treat home-based child care as socially valuable work to be rewarded from the social fund. There is of course plenty of room for debate about whether this would be desirable in practice, and there are alternatives which would be equally compatible with egalitarian principles, such as the universal provision of communal child care facilities (crèches etc.). There are large issues here, but they are not problems in principle for the notion of equality. Nor is Marx's further remark, that 'one has more children than another'. I assume that a consistent egalitarian policy would include the provision of adequate child allowances made over to those adults who were bringing up children. Again there might be complications in practice, such as the need for a population policy which discouraged large families, but such considerations do not make the idea of equality itself any less coherent.

Marx nevertheless insists on referring to these complications as 'defects', which are 'inevitable in the first phase of communist society'. He contrasts that 'first phase' with a later stage which he describes in a famous passage:

In a higher phase of communist society, after the enslaving subordination of the individual to the division of labour, and therewith also the antithesis between mental and physical labour, has vanished; after labour has become not only a means of life but life's prime want; after the productive forces have also increased with the all-round development of the individual, and all the springs of cooperative wealth flow more abundantly—only then can the narrow horizon of bourgeois right be crossed in its entirety and society inscribe on its banner: From each according to his ability, to each according to his needs! (p. 569)

This description is not very explicit, but it seems to imply that in a society of abundance, problems of distribution are transcended altogether. All members of the society can take whatever they need from the common stock of goods.

I do not find this convincing. It involves the extension of the principle 'To each according to his needs' from the provision of welfare services to all material goods. This extension ignores the real distinction between those goods. which can properly be said to be 'needed' and those which cannot. Basic food and clothing, a house to live in, medical care—these are 'needs' in a strict sense, necessary prerequisites for any worthwhile human life. There are, however, a great many other things which people would like to have but which they cannot plausibly be said to need. I need enough food and drink to keep me well-nourished and healthy, but I do not need fine wines and gourmet food. I need somewhere to live, and that means more than a cramped hovel, but it does not mean being able to stay in a villa in every part of the world where I would like to take a holiday. Outside the realm of 'needs' in the strict sense, 'To each according to his needs' must really mean 'To each according to his desires'—the free and unlimited availability of all goods on demand. There are obvious and far-reaching objections to such a principle. It rests on an assumption of total abundance, and even if we allow for the possibility of great advances in productive techniques, and for an end to the artificial stimulation of demand by advertising, such an assumption seems extremely optimistic. And even if goods could be produced in sufficient abundance to satisfy everyone's desire, this would involve a tremendous waste of the earth's limited resources. Moreover, if all goods were freely available, there would be no incentive to work, and even if we allow for the possibilities of making work more attractive, and for an increased sense of responsibility in a more co-operative society, it would be rash to rely on the assumption that incentives to work would no longer be necessary.[5]

Once we abandon the assumption of total abundance, some principle of distribution becomes necessary. If goods were to be available free without purchase, there would then have to be a system of rationing. Everyone would be entitled to so many books, so many records, so many free meals, so much jewellery, so many bottles of wine, etc. The drawback of such a system is that it leaves little room for individual choice, for the operation of preferences for goods of one kind rather than another. The desirable alternative is therefore to

[5] I have discussed in chapter 4 the place of the idea of 'incentives' within a theory of equality.

retain the use of money or something like it, enabling people to buy what goods they please. We are thus returned to Marx's 'first phase', which seems after all to be a better account of egalitarian justice than he himself allows.

An adequate account of 'equality of wealth' must, then, retain some distinction between the communal provision of goods for people's basic needs, and other goods which are purchased by individuals according to their personal preferences. Though I have said that there is an inescapable division between goods which are needed and those which are merely wanted, there is in practice plenty of room for flexibility in determining which goods should be freely available and which should be purchased.[6] A good contemporary example of a controversial case is the debate about whether to provide free public transport. One can imagine, in due course, the free communal provision of housing and of basic foods. Egalitarians will, I think, tend to favour communal provision of goods to satisfy needs, where this is practically feasible. I maintain only that *some* division has to be made between these goods and others. So our elucidation of 'equality of wealth' comes down to something like this: 'Free communal provision of goods to satisfy everyone's basic needs, and, beyond that, the distribution of wealth in such a way that everyone benefits equally overall from the work of the community on condition that, if they are able to do so, they participate in such work.'

CULTURAL AND EDUCATIONAL OPPORTUNITIES

The equal provision of cultural and educational opportunities could perhaps have been included under the heading 'material goods'. I have already mentioned it in passing, quoting from Marx, as one of the welfare services for which communal provision is appropriate, and although what has to be provided in the sphere of education is more than just material goods in the narrow sense, the same is true of, for example, medical care. There is bound to be a certain arbitrariness in our drawing of the boundaries between different kinds of

---

[6] A characteristically sane discussion of the practical issues can be found in ch. 4 of Bertrand Russell, *Roads to Freedom* (London 1st edn. 1918 and frequently republished).

equality, but there are reasons for treating education as a separate category. Over the past few decades some egalitarians have, indeed, given it a special and honoured place. They have seen the pursuit of educational equality as the most important way of producing an egalitarian society. They have supposed that one could break down the rigid divisions between classes and between social groups by developing the educational system as a source of social mobility, giving everyone a chance to achieve success, whatever his or her background and origins. The ideal at work here is 'equality of opportunity' in the narrow sense which we have encountered previously. It is the idea of society as a race in which only a few can win the prizes but in which everyone can compete and can achieve according to his or her ability. Or, to change the metaphor, it is the conception of the educational system as a ladder, which everyone can try to climb, in an attempt to reach the social positions at the top. Success on one rung of the educational ladder, measured by competitive examinations, will enable one to climb to the next educational level. Everyone will be educated to the level of his or her abilities, and will then be able to obtain a job appropriate to those abilities.

By now the drawbacks are apparent. There are, in the first place, practical obstacles. It has come to be recognized that the educational system cannot by itself provide opportunities equally to all. Children who have been given a head start at home before they begin school, whose parents are themselves educated and articulate and are able to provide them with encouragement and self-confidence, are likely to make much better use of the opportunities which schooling makes available. Consequently social classes and groups tend to perpetuate themselves through the educational system; children with middle class parents tend to end up with middle class jobs, children with working class parents tend to get working class jobs, and the promised social mobility fails to materialize in any great degree.

One immediate response to the problem has been to propose a policy of 'positive discrimination' instead of simply making the same educational facilities available to all. In this country one version of such a policy has been to spend additional money on facilities in so-called 'educational priority areas'—likely to be inner-city areas with a low-income population, often racially mixed, in poor housing.[7] Another form of 'positive discrimination', attempted more in the United States, has been to give preference to candidates from disadvantaged groups when considering admissions to higher education. This may be formalized by setting numerical quotas—such-and-such a proportion of college entrants must be blacks, or such-and-such a proportion must be women. The consequence is, of course, that candidates from groups who are favoured by positive discrimination may be selected in preference to other candidates who are better qualified.[8]

Not surprisingly, the idea of positive discrimination has proved controversial. Adopted in the name of equality, it nevertheless seems to offend against the very idea of equality, since it requires that certain groups be given preferential treatment. I do not think that there necessarily has to be a problem here; it depends on what kind of justification is offered for positive discrimination. If it is presented as itself the embodiment of equality, it probably runs into incoherence. But if it is presented as a transitional measure, involving a kind of inequality now for the sake of greater equality in the future, it can, I think, be defended. The defence would rest on the claim that by being given preferential opportunities in education, a previously disadvantaged group may lose its low self-image, may acquire greater confidence as a group and break out of the cycle of deprivation. In some cases this factual claim seems plausible. Where there exists, for example, an assumption that the study of scientific subjects is inappropriate for women, it may help to undermine that assumption if preferential consideration is given to women candidates, encouraging women to become scientists now so that they may serve as models for the next generation and establish the normality of the practice. The same may be true of racial groups. Positive discrimination now to get blacks

[7] The policy was advocated in the 'Plowden Report': *Children and their Primary Schools: A Report of the Central Advisory Council for Education* (London 1967). See especially ch. 5.

[8] For a useful introduction to the issues and the literature concerning positive discrimination (or 'reverse discrimination') see Singer, *Practical Ethics* ch. 2, pp. 40–7, and the further references which he gives.

into higher education may make it easier for blacks to acquire higher education in the future without the need for positive discrimination.

Although positive discrimination may, then, help to eliminate certain kinds of racial and sexual inequality, there are other kinds of inequality which it cannot change—and this for reasons which return us to the inadequacy of the narrow concept of equal opportunity. We may in this way be able to prevent the division between racial groups or the division between the sexes from coinciding with the division between the privileged and the deprived sections of society, but we cannot in the same way eliminate privilege and deprivation. Where the basic structure of a society is one of inequality, equality of educational opportunity may enable some people to rise up the educational ladder to positions of wealth and power, but, necessarily, it cannot enable everyone to do so. Not everyone can get to the top; if some climb from lower positions to higher, others must descend to fill the positions left empty. In an unequal society, then, this version of equal opportunity can only be what Tawney calls 'a lightning-conductor'—a way of reconciling people to their deprivation by holding out the prospect that some few may be able to escape it.[9]

We have seen however that there is another and a wider version of equality of opportunity, the idea that, in so far as social arrangements can achieve it, everyone should have an equal opportunity of enjoying a worthwhile life. This too cannot be achieved solely by means of an educational system, but it does have implications for the organization of education, since there are particular ways in which education can create opportunities for a worthwhile life. Thus, within the sphere of education, equality of opportunity can be taken to mean equal opportunities for everyone to develop their abilities to the full. Tawney puts it in this way:

What a wise parent would desire for his own children, that a nation, in so far as it is wise, must desire for all children. Educational equality consists in securing it for them. It is to be achieved in school, as it is achieved in the home, by recognizing that

[9] Tawney, *Equality* ch. 3 (ii), p. 103.

there are diversities of gifts, which require for their development diversities of treatment. Its aim will be to do justice to all, by providing facilities which are at once various in type and equal in quality. (p. 146)

The achievement of this educational goal will still be limited by features of the wider society. Children from one social class and family background will be in a better position to develop their abilities than will children from another class and background, even if they are provided with equally good educational facilities. Positive discrimination in the form of special provision for certain schools may be justified, but there is a limit to what it can achieve. Moreover, however much we may assert that it is equally important for each child to develop his or her abilities, whatever those abilities may be, the fact remains that certain kinds of abilities are more socially and economically advantageous to their possessor than others. One individual may have the ability to become a top surgeon, another may have the ability to grow roses; both abilities are worth developing and each may be equally satisfying to its possessor, but in an unequal society a top surgeon is likely to earn a good deal more than a gardener, and someone with the ability to become the former is therefore likely to have a good deal more encouragement and incentive to develop his or her abilities. Here as elsewhere, we see the close interlinking between the various kinds of equality and inequality, and the impossibility of creating an egalitarian society simply by pursuing equality in education.

Nevertheless, in so far as one can confine one's attention within the sphere of education, the idea of equal opportunity for each individual to develop his or her abilities does seem to me to be a coherent egalitarian ideal. It recognizes the diversity of people's skills and talents, and the fact that not everyone will need the same kind of education. It is therefore not open to the charge often made, that the pursuit of equality in education is tantamount to the pursuit of mediocrity. Egalitarians, it is said, since they obviously cannot raise everyone to the level of the ablest learners, are bound to pull everyone down to the level of the least able. That accusation results from retaining the concept of the educational ladder and supposing that if something stronger is sought than the principle of giving everyone equal opportunity to try to reach the top, it will have to be the requirement that everyone should be on the same rung. That, however, is not the kind of equality which we are considering. The wider notion of equality of opportunity is one which dispenses with the 'ladder' concept altogether, which recognizes that different people have different kinds of abilities and which maintains that each individual has an equal need to develop his or her abilities in order to lead a worthwhile life.

A further consequence of abandoning the 'ladder' metaphor is that we cease to see education as a sequence of predetermined stages attached to particular ages of childhood and youth. We can recognize that the development of talents and skills is something which people need to pursue or return to at different times of their lives, as their interests and perceptions change and as they discover new abilities. 'Adult education' may cease to be regarded as a minor appendage and become instead an integral part of a continuing process. Given the practical limits on the proportion of a society's resources which can be devoted to education, we should perhaps think in terms of an equal and automatic entitlement to so many years' free education, which people can decide to use at whatever time of life they choose.

I have been stressing the diversity of people's talents and interests, but I do not want to put all the emphasis on differences between individuals. Just as important for educational equality, I think, is the idea of a common culture and the role of education in creating this common culture and giving everyone access to it.[10] To speak of a common culture is not to rule out the existence of a diversity of local and regional cultures, of ethnic traditions and sub-cultures. Underlying this diversity, however, at a more fundamental level, it is important that a society should possess shared traditions, a sense of a common history, a shared language of moral and political debate, shared values, and a literature

[10] In thinking about the idea of a 'common culture' and its connection with education, I am much influenced by the work of Raymond Williams; see his *Culture and Society* (London 1958 and Harmondsworth, 1961), especially the Conclusion, and *The Long Revolution* (London 1961 and Harmondsworth, 1965) Part 2, ch. 1.

which embodies and expresses them. It is important that all the members of the society should have access to this culture and should be able to experience it as their own. Its importance is closely connected with the idea of equality of power and the need for a genuinely participatory democracy. These cannot exist if, whatever the formal political rights possessed by ordinary people, the real political debates take place within a narrow circle of people who, united among themselves by a privileged educational background, appropriate to themselves the culture of their society. The notion of a common culture is a difficult one to pin down precisely, but I can perhaps help to illuminate it in a negative way by pointing to a direct expression of the breakdown of a common culture in our own society—the situation of the press. There has long existed a division between the so-called 'quality' press in which, for all its limitations, important issues are raised and discussed about the present state and future direction of our society, and the 'popular' press in which such issues sometimes get an airing but are all too often buried beneath a mountain of trivia. This division does not represent a healthy diversity, nor is it an authentic expression of the sub-cultures of different classes. Those who write for and edit the popular press do not themselves share the sub-culture of their readers; they are engaged in a process of manipulation which actively excludes most people from the dominant culture and from rational political debate. The contrast between the 'quality' and 'popular' press is thus a symptom of the absence of a common culture, and an indication of the link between this and inequality of power.

If educational equality requires a common culture, then it requires also a common educational system; the latter is a necessary means to the former. This has obvious implications for the controversial question of whether a public education system should co-exist with private educational institutions (I use the terms 'public' and 'private' in their accurate sense; the so-called 'public' schools of this country are private educational institutions). I do not want to enter into the details of this controversy, but only to note two egalitarian arguments for the abolition of separate private education. The first is a severely practical argument. If education can be privately purchased, it will be bought by the wealthier, more powerful, and more influential sections of a society. Those same sections of society, if they had to share a publicly funded and publicly administered education system, would devote their wealth, power, and influence to ensuring that the public system was the best possible. The co-existence of public and private education thus lowers the quality of the public education, and exacerbates educational inequalities.

The second argument would be one which links the question of public and private education with that of a common culture. The existence of a separate private sector in education not only depresses the quality of the public educational system; it also, in a more general way, creates a separate culture. It destroys the possibility of a common culture in the sense which I have tried to indicate. It thereby exacerbates inequalities of power; a class or group which has a large share of formal power is able, by purchasing a separate education, to create its own minority culture which makes effective power even more remote from other sections of society.

Of course this argument, like the previous one, presupposes the existence of inequalities of power and wealth, and it might be said that neither objection to private education would apply if there were no such inequalities. Strictly speaking that may be true; but the fact is that anything approaching perfect equality of power and of wealth is immensely difficult to achieve. There will, in any society, be *some* tendency towards such inequalities, and a divided educational system will always magnify that tendency, by enabling those who have more power and more wealth to form a separate and self-perpetuating group.

I take the concrete elements of equality, then, to be a radical participatory democracy, the common ownership and democratic control of economic institutions, the communal provision of welfare services, parity of incomes, and a common educational system giving everyone the opportunity of developing his or her abilities to the full. The list may seem wildly utopian. I shall have a little more to say about the charge of utopianism in a later chapter. Meanwhile I make no apology for the fact that my account of an egalitarian society does not describe any existing society. Equality is a goal which has been much discussed but only very imperfectly achieved. Nevertheless, the concrete features of a society of equality which I have listed are not dreamed up out of nowhere. They are not just a philosopher's musings. They are the goals for which egalitarian political movements have striven in practice. And though those movements have made only limited progress, it has been progress none the less. In our own society, over the past century, something has been achieved on all these fronts. It is not necessarily a criticism of an ideal that it cannot be perfectly realized, provided it can be effectively aimed at and can serve as a standard to which actual societies can at least approximate.

I make no claim to originality, then, in my account of the features of a society of equality. They are the familiar aims of egalitarian movements. What I have tried to do is to explain what their connection is with equality, why they follow from that general idea, and how together they make up a coherent and feasible social ideal. I also think that by specifying in this way the concrete features of an egalitarian society we are in a better position to meet some of the objections to equality. In the next chapter I shall turn to those objections which are the main theme of this book, objections having to do with the alleged incompatibility between freedom and equality. Meanwhile I want to conclude the present chapter by mentioning briefly one other common objection, the charge that to pursue equality is to aim at a 'levelling-down' of everyone to a common mediocrity. We have already seen that this charge is especially made within the sphere of education, where it is suggested that egalitarians want to prevent the most talented children from developing their talents to the full because they would then outshine their less able fellows. But the same charge is also made more generally—that the ideal of equality would require us to prevent people from enjoying happy and successful lives, because they would then be superior to others.

Now of course no sane egalitarian will want mere equality. The egalitarian goal is not just equal well-being (in so far as it can be promoted by social arrangements), but maximum equal well-being. It is not just that all the members of a co-operative community should benefit equally, but also that they should all benefit as much as possible. The problems arise, of course, when the goals of equalizing the benefits and of maximizing the benefits conflict. It may be that some members of the community can be made better-off, but only in ways which will enable them to benefit more than others and will thus create inequalities. What are we to say then? In so far as such conflicts can be brought under any general principle, the appropriate egalitarian principle will, I think, be Rawls's 'difference principle': social and economic inequalities are justified only if they are to the greatest benefit of the least advantaged.[11] This principle is essentially egalitarian, as I have argued in chapter 4, because it is one on which everybody could agree in a co-operative community. What cannot be justified, from an egalitarian point of view, are social arrangements which benefit some only by making other people worse off than they would otherwise have been.

That, then, will be the appropriate general principle to adjudicate the conflict between equalizing benefits and maximizing benefits. At this point, however, I want to connect the general principle with the three components of equality which I have listed, for it will have importantly different implications when brought to bear on those various components. The case of material goods seems straightforward: greater material rewards for some are justified if they increase the material benefits of even the least well-off. The only question then is the empirical one: will the least well-off in fact be benefitted by such inequalities? I have already registered my scepticism about the need for 'incentives' to induce people to perform skilled and responsible jobs which benefit everyone. I doubt whether the Rawlsian principle will in practice justify very greater material inequalities, but as a principle it seems at any rate to make sense when applied to material goods.

Much the same is true of educational equalities and inequalities. No doubt some people are capable of developing

---

[11] As we have seen, this is only the first half of the principle, which continues: '. . . and attached to offices and positions open to all under conditions of fair equality of opportunity'.

their abilities more than others, and to do so they may require more educational resources than others either could, or would want to, make use of. The egalitarian need not object to their being given such resources, especially since this may enable them to develop talents which will be of value to the community as a whole. Not everyone can make use of higher education, but that is no reason for preventing those who can from doing so. Egalitarians will, however, object to the more able being given additional resources if this makes it more difficult for the less able children to develop even such abilities as they have.

The picture becomes more complicated when we consider the interplay between material goods and educational resources. It is at least arguable that by giving additional educational resources to the most talented, we might decrease the educational resources for the less able but indirectly increase their material benefits. A drive to step up the training of engineers or information-technologists, for example, might mean a decline in provision for other areas of education, it might mean more children leaving school without having achieved a basic literacy, but it might also in the long run help to achieve greater material comforts for everyone. What is the egalitarian to say? I doubt whether there is anything very illuminating that can be said at the general level. One must allow, I think, that such trade-offs can in principle be justified, and the rest will depend on the particular case. One can only add that it is important not to undervalue education in comparison with material goods. In particular—and this will be very important from the egalitarian point of view— the lack of an effective education may prevent people from playing an active part in the life of their community, and that is not something which can be compensated for by any amount of material comforts.

At this point the question of equality in education verges on that of equality of power, and that is where Rawls's principle becomes inoperative. Power, unlike material goods and educational resources, is essentially relational. In the sense in which I have been talking about it—social power, not mere technical mastery of things—unequal power is always power over other people. To the extent that A has greater power over B, B necessarily has less power. Consequently it could not, in principle, be the case that greater inequalities of power increased the power of the least powerful. Rawls's principle cannot justify inequalities of power on such grounds.

What about trade-offs between power and wealth? What if inequalities of power could produce greater wealth for all, including the least well-off? That is indeed a claim that is made. Some would maintain that, at least in certain societies or at certain stages of economic development, the firm rule of a benevolent despot or dictator or a ruling élite would make for greater economic efficiency than a more democratic regime. More cautiously, it might be said that at least economic institutions themselves will function more effectively if the technical experts are given a free hand without having to be answerable at every turn to workers' councils or the like. What we decide about such cases will again depend in part on how we assess the empirical claims; against the skills of the experts we have to set the economic advantages which stem from the greater involvement and commitment of ordinary workers. But what if, in some cases, the empirical claims can be made good and inequalities of power really will work to the economic advantage of everyone? Should these inequalities be accepted? As before, it is difficult to make any general judgement. A rational egalitarian is, I think, bound to accept some such trade-offs. At the same time, there is a definite limit to what can be accepted, a limit which is hard to locate precisely but which is none the less important. Beyond a certain point, inequalities of power will make it impossible to talk any longer of a co-operative community, however great the material prosperity which everyone enjoys. At that point the idea of equality will have been sacrificed altogether. This is so because, as I have been maintaining, equality of power is the most basic kind of equality, the one which determines the overall character of the community.

# 7

# Freedom versus Equality?

So far I have dealt separately with the concepts of 'freedom' and 'equality'. In each case I have tried to explain why each is an important value by showing how each is rooted in human experience, in basic human needs and aspirations. From that vantage point I have then attempted to show what each of these values properly consists in. I turn now to the relation between them, and to the claim made by many of the opponents of equality, that freedom and equality are incompatible values. The pursuit of equality will, it is often suggested, lead to the imposing of a straitjacket on society and to the crushing of individual liberty. What are we to say to this?[1]

[1] A good deal has been said already by previous writers. I quoted in chapter 1 Hume's assertion of the incompatibility of freedom and equality. Influential recent writers in the same vein include F. A. Hayek (see for example his *The Constitution of Liberty* (London 1960), especially ch. 6); Milton Friedman (e.g. his *Capitalism and Freedom* (Chicago and London 1962) ch. 10, and Milton and Rose Friedman, *Free to Choose* (Harmondsworth 1980) ch. 5; and Robert Nozick, *Anarchy, State and Utopia* (New York 1974), especially Part II. A similar position is shared by many of the contributors to *Against Equality*, ed. William Letwin (London 1983). The political impact of this position is indicated by the fact that it has been defended by a recent member of a Conservative government; see Keith Joseph and Jonathan Sumption, *Equality* (London 1979), especially ch. 3. The opposed position, which I shall defend, treating freedom and equality not as incompatible but as interconnected values, has been stated in R. H. Tawney, *Equality* (4th edn.), especially chs. 5 (ii) and 7 (iii), and in E. F. Carritt, 'Liberty and Equality', *Law Quarterly Review*, vol. 56 (1940), reprinted in *Political Philosophy*, ed. Anthony Quinton (Oxford 1967). More recently, Michael Walzer, in *Spheres of Justice: A Defence of Pluralism and Equality* (Oxford 1983), and Kai Nielsen, in *Equality and Liberty: A Defense of Radical Egalitarianism* (New Jersey 1985) have developed theories of equality which aim to exhibit the concordance of freedom and equality. The influence of such thinking in Labour Party circles is apparent in Raymond Plant, *Equality, Markets and the State* (Fabian Society pamphlet no. 494, London 1984), in Bryan Gould, *Socialism and Freedom* (London 1985), and indeed in sections of Neil Kinnock's lecture on 'The Future of Socialism', published as Fabian Society pamphlet no. 509 (London 1986). I have discussed Walzer and Plant in a review article in *Radical Philosophy* 39 (1985). My own previous attempts to sort out the relation between freedom and equality are 'Does Equality Destroy Liberty?', in Keith Graham (ed.) *Contemporary Political Philosophy*, (Cambridge 1982), and 'Liberty, Equality, Property', in *Aristotelian Society Supplementary Volume 55* (1981); the latter article

Much of what I want to say will, I hope, be already apparent. The claim that freedom and equality are incompatible is often made to depend on an understanding of 'equality' which is simply a caricature. I have stressed in chapter 5, for instance, that the ideal of equality is not to be identified with a desire to eliminate differences between individuals. Equality is not the same thing as uniformity, and no advocate of equality, as far as I know, has ever suggested that it is. Anti-egalitarians, however, are all too ready to identify the two. Thus F. A. Hayek insists that 'the boundless variety of human nature—the wide range of differences in individual capacities and potentialities—is one of the most distinctive facts about the human species'.[2] From this incontrovertible premiss he infers that 'as a statement of fact, it just is not true that "all men are born equal"'. Equality before the law, which he regards as the only acceptable version of the ideal of equality, will require that all human beings are treated alike despite these differences between them. Any stronger version of equality, however, any attempt to achieve what he calls 'material equality', will involve the aim of eliminating these natural differences between people, and will therefore inevitably be coercive. Hayek then concludes that 'the desire of making people more alike in their condition cannot be accepted in a free society as a justification for further and discriminatory coercion'.[3]

This argument is sufficiently answered by pointing out that the ideal of equality is *not* 'the desire of making people more alike in their condition'. It is, as we have seen, the desire that all the members of a community should as far as possible be equal in the power that they wield, should benefit equally from the material advantages made available through the community, and should have equal access to the educational opportunities and cultural life of the community. Such an ideal is entirely compatible with an immense variety between individuals. Equality of power is compatible with differentiation of function. Equality of material welfare is compatible with individual choice of the goods and activities to be

was very helpfully stimulated by David Lloyd Thomas's contribution to the same symposium.

[2] *The Constitution of Liberty* p. 86.        [3] Ibid. p. 87.

enjoyed. Equality in education is compatible with diversity in people's aptitudes and abilities. The egalitarian ideal is emphatically not one of imposing a straitjacket on people's varied roles, talents, and idiosyncracies. That would indeed be inimical to freedom, but it is not required by equality.

We can go further. The results of the previous chapters support the view that freedom and equality, far from being opposed ideals, actually coincide. That view, as we noted in the introductory chapter, has been distinctive of one particular tradition of political thought and action, and it has also an intuitive plausibility. People and movements struggling against what they see as 'oppression' may with equal appropriateness present their struggle as a struggle for 'freedom' or as a struggle for 'equality'. I think that we are now in a position to identify in more detail the connections between the two concepts. We saw in chapters 2 and 3 that it is not possible to describe what constitutes a 'free society' by distinguishing between the respective spheres of 'the individual' and 'society' and by requiring that the individual should be left alone by society. No such absolute dividing line can be drawn. Freedom does not just mean being left alone, it depends upon positive conditions which are socially created and socially assigned. Hence, if we are to apply the epithet 'free' to a whole society, we have to consider how these positive conditions of freedom are distributed within that society, and the society will be a free society to the extent that those conditions are distributed equally rather than enjoyed disproportionately by particular sections of the society. This, then, is the first step in the linking of freedom and equality.

Turning then to the discussion of equality in general, I argued in chapter 4 that equality is to be defended as the form of distributive justice appropriate to a co-operative community, and that what is distinctive of a co-operative community is that it is the form of association in which people relate to one another as free participants in a common enterprise. Thus the value of freedom is centrally invoked in the argument for equality. In chapters 5 and 6 I then suggested that the major components of equality are equality of power, equality of material wealth, and equality of educational opportunities. These are the three factors which we also identified as the most important positive conditions of freedom. Consequently, a society of equality will be one in which the conditions of freedom are distributed equally. The more people share equally in power, wealth, and educational opportunities, the more they will then share equally also in freedom, and the more truly their society can then be described as a 'free society'. The link between freedom and equality is thus established from both directions.

Now this may look altogether too neat. The reader may suspect it to be a mere conjuring-trick, a sleight of hand which conceals real problems and conflicts. I do, in fact, agree that there may be real dilemmas within the egalitarian ideal, dilemmas which the anti-egalitarian argument may bring to our attention, albeit in a confused way. I shall try to suggest what these dilemmas are, but I shall also argue that they are misdescribed and oversimplified when they are presented as a conflict between the (good) ideal of freedom and the (bad) ideal of equality.

Consider the following example of such a presentation. Antony Flew, in his article 'The Procrustean Ideal: Libertarians v. Egalitarians', argues that 'there has to be compulsion if everyone is to be got and kept either up or down, as individually appropriate, to the officially approved average level of whatever it may be which is being equalised' (p. 160).[4] There are, he claims, 'good general reasons to believe that a strenuous, sustained and extensive policy for imposing the ideal . . . will as a matter of fact call for a highly authoritarian and widely repressive form of government' (p. 162). He then comments:

even in the somewhat unlikely event that such an uncriticisable and irremovable Power Elite were to subdue all temptations to appropriate massive prerequisites (sic) and privileges for its own members, still its absolute power over, and its total control of, the rest of society must in itself constitute the greatest possible offence to any genuine ideal either of personal equality or even of equality of outcome. (p. 163)

Ironically, Flew's argument has overreached itself. He explicitly

---

[4] References are to *Against Equality*, ed. William Letwin (see note 1 above), where the article is reprinted. It originally appeared in *Encounter* vol. 50, no. 3 (1978).

recognizes that such a state of affairs would be contrary not only to the ideal of freedom but also to the ideal of equality itself. At most, then, what he points us to is a conflict within the ideal of equality. That conflict would, if it exists, be between equality of power and equality of wealth. It may be that a thoroughgoing equality of wealth could be achieved only by an authority which concentrated power in its own hands. If a choice then has to be made between equality of power and equality of wealth, the former is, I have previously argued, the more basic ingredient of the egalitarian ideal.

Whether there is such a conflict is an empirical question, and one which must finally be decided not by broad empirical generalizations but by the detailed experience of practical politics. If the conflict does arise, it is likely to take the form of a tension between the centralizing and the decentralizing strands within egalitarian politics. Equality of power, I have suggested, must mean a radical democracy; this may require the devolution of power to workplaces and to localities, and this in turn *may* give rise to material inequalities between different sectors of the economy or between different regions. If region A is more favoured in its natural resources than region B, and if, in the interests of democracy, the inhabitants of each region have a large measure of control over their economic activities, the inhabitants of A may achieve greater prosperity than the inhabitants of B. It may be that this inequality could be avoided only by a more centralized control of the economy.

Flew himself has, however, provided grounds for scepticism even about the empirical claim. He has described it as 'unlikely' that a power élite would resist the temptation to amass privileges for itself. He is, in other words, rightly impressed by the familiar dictum that all power tends to corrupt. A power élite might, in good faith, set itself the task of creating a more equal distribution of material goods, and might even make real progress in that direction. But even if the first generation of equalizers were to remain true to their ideal, it is unlikely that future generations could be relied upon to do so. In the long run a self-perpetuating élite is likely to arrogate to itself a monopoly of material privileges. It may well be, then, that the only secure basis for equality of wealth is equality of power. In practice, at any rate, the genuine egalitarian will give priority to equality of power, and will strive for the achievement of a democratically agreed equality of wealth, but not at the expense of equality of power.

There remains one further argument which we need to consider at some length: the suggestion that the pursuit of equality will at any rate override one particular class of freedoms which are identifiable as basic human rights. The idea here is that the concept of 'rights' serves to mark out the most important and most valuable kinds of freedom, which have a special protected status, and the violation of which is therefore especially serious from a moral point of view. In particular, it is sometimes suggested that property rights have this kind of status, and that the attempt to make people more equal, whatever other consequences it may have for freedom in some wider sense, is bound to override that basic freedom which consists in the right to do what one likes with one's own property. We need, therefore, to look more closely at the concept of rights, and in due course also at the specific concept of property rights, to determine whether these concepts throw any new light on the relations between freedom and equality.

The concept of rights which we are talking about here is that of so-called moral rights, and that idea is in itself a problematic one. It is to be contrasted with the much less problematic notion of conventional rights, rights which are assigned to people by laws or by other social institutions. Such rights are sometimes also called 'positive' rights. Consider the statement that the citizens of the United States have the right to more information about the activities of their government than do the citizens of Britain. The truth of this statement can be determined simply by looking at the constitutions, laws, and political arrangements of the two countries. It just is a fact that their laws are different in this respect, and that in consequence the rights of the citizens of the one country are different from those of the other. But now consider the statement: 'Everyone has a right to know what their own government is doing'. As a statement of fact about existing legal and institutional arrangements, this is plainly false. Some countries curtail this right more than others, and some curtail it altogether. Nevertheless the statement is one which is made, and those who make it would say that they are not intending to state a fact about existing laws and institutions; they are asserting a moral right. They are saying something about what ought to be the case, and the existence of this moral right is itself taken to be grounds for criticizing the absence of the corresponding conventional or positive right. 'Everyone has a right to such information', they are saying, 'and that is what is wrong with countries which deny it.'

*Can* there be moral rights in this sense?[5] How could we establish that there are? It has sometimes been suggested that such rights are 'self-evident'. The American Declaration of Independence stated in 1776: 'We hold these truths to be self-evident, that all men are created equal; that they are endowed by their Creator with certain unalienable rights; that among these are life, liberty, and the pursuit of happiness'. The idea of 'self-evidence', however, should always be regarded with suspicion. In the absence of at least some further explanation, it looks like a piece of dogmatism, a refusal to give reasons when reasons are called for. Can anything better then be offered?

Developing the contrast with conventional rights, these basic moral rights have also traditionally been described as 'natural rights'. This in turn has sometimes led to their being seen as the rights which human beings would have in a 'state of nature'. The idea of a 'state of nature' belongs within the tradition of thought which sees social institutions as resting upon some kind of 'social contract' (a tradition which is also developed in a very different direction by the work of John Rawls which we considered in chapter 4). Seventeenth- and eighteenth-century writers in the 'social contract' tradition

---

[5] There can certainly be moral rights in other, less interesting senses. These are the moral rights involved in various specific moral roles and relationships. For example, if someone has promised to give me something, I have a moral right to it (whether or not this right is legally or socially upheld). That is part of the moral understanding of what it is to be the recipient of a promise. The distinctive feature of the 'basic' moral rights which we are considering in this chapter is that they are held not just to belong to the occupants of particular moral positions but to be universal, belonging to human beings as such; and that is what is problematic about them.

described human beings living in a state of nature, without any established social institutions or system of government, and then coming together to make a contract with one another establishing the system of rules and authority which would constitute 'civil society'. Some of these writers, such as the seventeenth-century British philosopher John Locke, then suggest that there are certain basic rights which human beings would have enjoyed in the state of nature, that the contract to enter into civil society would have been made by them only if it guaranteed these basic rights, and that therefore any existing society which fails to respect such rights is incapable of justifying its existence, since it has failed to measure up to the essential requirements of a human society.[6]

The difficulties with this theory of natural rights are legion. The classical theories of 'the social contract' are typically written as though they were accounts of an actual historical event, yet there is no evidence whatever that such an event ever took place—a fact frequently acknowledged by the writers themselves, whose narratives must therefore be read as purely hypothetical accounts of what a state of nature would be like if it were to exist, and what form the social contract would take if human beings in a state of nature had to make an agreement to found a society. The hypothetical interpretation, however, makes the theory an even more precarious basis for an account of natural rights. How can we possibly determine what rights people would have in a state of nature, if such a condition is a purely imaginary one? There are no apparent constraints determining what rights we may choose to ascribe to them. Anything goes, and it is not surprising that the defenders of natural rights cannot agree on what these rights are. (Locke has 'life, liberty, and property'; the American Declaration of Independence has 'life, liberty, and the pursuit of happiness'; the Declaration of the Rights of Man and of Citizens, formulated by the French National Assembly in 1789, has 'liberty, property, security, and resistance to oppression'.)

---

[6] Locke's theory is set out in his *Second Treatise of Civil Government* (1690), though he uses the terminology of 'natural rights' surprisingly rarely. Much less sophisticated, but much more explicit in defence of natural rights, is Tom Paine, *The Rights of Man* (1781).

Any ascription of rights to human beings in a state of nature seems, then, to be entirely arbitrary. Why? Perhaps because the very idea is meaningless. The notion of a 'right' means nothing unless it means a power which is in some way guaranteed—guaranteed, that is, by some institution or convention. Hence the idea of rights in a state of nature is a contradiction. That is the view forcibly expressed by Jeremy Bentham in 1795 when, commenting on the French Declaration of Rights, he wrote:

How stands the truth of things? That there are no such things as natural rights—no such things as rights anterior to the establishment of government—no such things as natural rights opposed to, in contradistinction to, legal: that the expression is merely figurative. . . . We know what it is for men to live without government—and living without government, to live without rights . . . no government, and thence no laws—no laws, and thence no such things as rights—no security—no property:—liberty, as against regular control, the control of laws and government—perfect; but as against all irregular control, the mandates of stronger individuals, none.[7]

Natural rights, he concludes, 'is simple nonsense: natural and imprescriptible rights, rhetorical nonsense,—nonsense upon stilts'.

The same line of reasoning, we might add, reveals the impossibility not only of ascribing rights to human beings in a state of nature, but of attributing to such beings any distinctively human activities at all. In particular, beings isolated from one another in a state of nature could not possess a language, and therefore could not reason or deliberate; nor, for that matter, could they ever be in a position to form a social contract. Not only does the hypothesis of a state of nature fail to illuminate the concept of rights, it is quite generally a useless fiction.

If the hypothesis of a state of nature cannot establish the existence of moral rights, it is difficult to see how any other 'natural' facts about human beings could do so. 'Social'

---

[7] Jeremy Bentham, *Anarchical Fallacies*, in *Works*, ed. John Bowring (London 1843, and New York 1962), p. 500, and reprinted in A. I. Melden (ed.) *Human Rights*, (Belmont 1970), p. 31. Melden's is a useful collection of readings on the present topic.

facts—facts about people's social roles and positions—cannot do the job, for by definition what they would establish would be 'conventional', 'positive' rights, not moral rights. Are there any other plausible candidates? Suppose, let us say, that we were to appeal to facts about people's needs—for example, that people need security, and that therefore security is a basic human right. Does the fact that people need security really establish that they have a right to it? What seems much more appropriate is to suggest that because people need it, it ought to be a right; but then this must mean: it ought to be a conventional right. In other words, what we are saying is that because a basic level of security is an essential need of all human beings, every society ought to be organized in such a way as to guarantee to all its members the right to such security. Why then bring in moral rights at all? We can say all that we want to say, simply by referring to the facts about human needs and then inferring that people ought to have the corresponding positive rights. The point holds good not just for needs, but for any supposed ground of rights-claims. Let G be the supposed ground for a rights-claim; let M be the moral right which it is supposed to establish; and let C be the corresponding conventional right. The defenders of moral rights will say that because of G, people have the moral right M. This moral right, however, is no good to people unless it is recognized, that is, unless it becomes a conventional right C. The only reason, therefore, for using G to establish right M is in order to argue that people ought to have conventional right C. In that case, however, it would be simpler and less confusing to argue directly from G to the conclusion that people ought to have C. The reference to the supposed moral right M is entirely redundant, a quite unnecessary intermediary between G and C. To regard it as a necessary step must be to assume that we cannot establish that people ought to have any conventional right unless in some sense they already (implicitly) have it (as a moral right). In other words, the idea seems to be that we cannot show that rights ought to be recognized on earth unless we can show that they are already recognized in heaven. This is confusing nonsense.

We can perhaps bring out these points more clearly by

applying them to the particular case of property rights. Can there be natural rights to property? The classic defence of the idea is made by Locke, who suggests that we acquire a natural right to something by mixing our labour with it.

Though the earth and all inferior creatures be common to all men, yet every man has a property in his own person; this nobody has any right to but himself. The labour of his body and the work of his hands we may say are properly his. Whatsoever, then, he removes out of the state that nature hath provided and left it in, he hath mixed his labour with, and joined to it something that is his own, and thereby makes it his property. It being by him removed from the common state nature placed it in, it hath by this labour something annexed to it that excludes the common right of other men. For this labour being the unquestionable property of the labourer, no man but he can have a right to what that is once joined to, at least where there is enough, and as good left in common for others. (*Second Treatise of Civil Government*, para. 27)

There are two main components in this argument: the claim that I have a natural right to own my own person; and the claim that when I work on something, this natural right is somehow extended to incorporate the object on which I work. Consider these two claims in turn. Surely, it may be said, I must own my own person; how could I not do so? How indeed. The trouble is that the relation between 'I' and 'my own person' is too close a relation; if we are to talk of ownership here, then nothing could conceivably count as my not owning it. It makes sense to talk about something as 'my property' only if it is something which I might or might not have owned—something, that is, which is distinct from me. 'My person' is not like that. It does not just belong to me, it *is* me. Of course there is a sense in which I can lose the ownership of myself. I may, for instance, become a slave, the property of a slave owner. But then in that sense my ownership of my own person is *not* a natural right. There is an inescapable dilemma here. Either my relation to my own person is so close that it cannot be destroyed by slavery, in which case it is too close a relation to be properly called 'ownership' at all; or we are talking about some looser relation, in which case it is too loose to establish a natural right of ownership, since it is a relation which may or may not hold.

However, even if I were to have a natural right to the ownership of my own person, it remains quite unexplained how this could be transferred to the objects on which I labour. We seem to be dealing with some kind of magical idea here—as though 'being an object of ownership' were some mysterious and unseen quality which, when I work on things, somehow passes through me and into them.

Now it may be objected that this is a caricature, and that the idea can be made much more plausible. Indeed it can, but notice how. It is made more plausible by supplying a context, and Locke in fact supplied one in the paragraph previous to the one which I quoted. There he argued that 'the earth and all that is therein is given to men for the support and comfort of their being', and that accordingly, if these things are 'given for the use of men, there must of necessity be a means to appropriate them some way or other before they can be of any use or at all beneficial to any particular man'. This, however, if it *is* given due weight, quite transforms the argument. The suggestion seems to be that human beings cannot make effective use of things unless they divide them up amongst themselves and treat them as property. In other words, the claim is not that the fact that someone has mixed his labour with a thing is, by itself, a reason for regarding it as his property; rather, the claim is that human beings need some way of dividing things up into private property, and the criterion of 'mixing one's labour' seems a convenient way of doing it. Now, however, we can bring our previous general point into play. If the above argument is a good argument at all, it is an argument for why 'mixing one's labour' *ought* to be regarded as establishing property rights. It ought to, because that is a convenient way of ensuring that things are effectively appropriated for human use. The argument becomes plausible, then, not as the claim that natural property rights are in fact established in this way, but as the claim that conventional property rights ought to be established in this way. When it is interpreted in this way, it can be properly assessed, for we can then recognize the possibility that there might be other and better ways of making use of the earth's resources, and therefore other and better ways of demarcating property. These possibilities are obscured by the talk of 'natural rights', which carries the implication that the 'labour' criterion simply settles the question of ownership.

It seems to me, then, that in all discussions of rights the introduction of 'natural rights' or 'basic moral rights' is an unnecessary redundancy, which simply confuses the issue. Ideally I would want to suggest that we drop the concept altogether. Unfortunately its use has become so entrenched that such a recommendation is unlikely to get very far. If we are to continue to talk of 'moral rights', however, it is at any rate essential to recognize that what we have here is a derivative ethical concept, not a fundamental one. The appeal to 'moral rights' does not by itself settle anything. The concept acquires whatever force it has from the more fundamental ethical considerations which are adduced as grounds for such rights. At best, then, talk of 'moral rights' is a shorthand way of talking about certain basic human needs or requirements which are so important that they ought to be recognized as positive rights in all societies.

All of this is crucial when we come to look at the claim that the pursuit of equality overrides people's rights. As we noted, the suggestion is likely to be that even if the pursuit of equality promotes the conditions of freedom in some wider sense, or promotes the fulfilment of other needs and aspirations, this must not be done at the expense of rights. The term 'rights' is typically used to pick out certain specific conditions of freedom and to give them a special protected status. Often these will be negative conditions of freedom—rights of non-interference—and in particular they are liable to include property rights, supposed rights not to be prevented from doing what one chooses with one's own property. But now the point is that merely calling them 'rights' is not enough to give them any special status. We have to look at the more fundamental ethical considerations which are held to establish such rights. We may then find that they do not after all have any special privileged status. They may turn out to be no more fundamental than the other conditions of freedom, or the other kinds of needs and aspirations, with which they are held to conflict. We may then conclude that moral rights may, and sometimes should, be overridden by other equally important considerations. Alternatively we may argue, as some philosophers have done, that if we are going to talk about moral rights at all we must widen the category to include not only negative rights of non-interference such as property rights, but also positive rights such as a right to exercise political power, a right to a fair share in the material resources of one's own community, or a right to educational opportunities. Whatever we say here, the important point is that none of this can be settled simply by an appeal to the concept of rights. It can be settled only by an appeal to the further ethical considerations on which rights-claims rest.

I want now to illustrate these general points by looking at an influential recent example of the anti-egalitarian argument, Robert Nozick's book *Anarchy, State, and Utopia*. Nozick's criticisms are directed not just against equality but against any principle of distributive justice which takes the form of what he calls a 'patterned principle'. By this he means any principle which lays down some desirable pattern for the distribution of goods in a society. The category would include such principles as that goods should be distributed equally, or should be distributed according to people's needs, but also non-egalitarian principles such as that goods should be distributed to people according to their deserts, or according to their work, or according to their value to society. The application of any such principle will, according to Nozick, inevitably violate people's rights. Individuals are constantly engaging in innumerable voluntary transactions with one another (buying, selling, giving, exchanging etc.), and these transactions will always tend to change the distribution of their 'holdings' (to use Nozick's term). Consequently any attempt to establish a particular pattern of distribution will have to prevent people engaging in these voluntary transactions which would otherwise subvert the pattern. It will thus violate their rights. According to Nozick the only acceptable view of justice is what he calls the 'entitlement' theory: roughly speaking, any distribution of holdings will be a just distribution if it comes about through voluntary transfers from some previous just distribution.[8] Nozick sees this as a theory of justice which gives the central place to notions of people's rights and liberties; and liberty, he says, upsets patterns.

Although Nozick sees this as an objection to any patterned principle of justice, I shall concentrate on its application to the idea of equality. His is, then, a classic example of a theory which gives certain kinds of liberties a special status as rights, and then argues that the pursuit of equality is morally objectionable because it violates those rights. I have argued that any defence of moral rights must derive them from some more fundamental ethical consideration, and Nozick's account of rights is no exception. He appeals to 'the underlying Kantian principle that individuals are ends and not merely means; they may not be sacrificed or used for the achieving of other ends without their consent. Individuals are inviolable' (pp. 30–1). This principle, he thinks, generates a notion of rights as 'side-constraints'. Side-constraints on action are to be contrasted with goals of action. The notion of side-constraints is a notion of limits which must be observed in the pursuit of any goals. There are some things which, morally, one may not do to people, regardless of how much good could be achieved by doing them. The idea of rights as side-constraints is thus a non-utilitarian ethical idea. Respect for rights is not a positive good which we aim to maximize; it is a negative limit which we should observe. And that means, according to Nozick, that the violation of rights is not something which we can justify by arguing that it is balanced by the achievement of a greater good elsewhere. Respect for

---

[8] This *is* a simplification. Two points call for comment. (a) What Nozick actually says is: 'A distribution is just if it arises from another just distribution by legitimate means. The legitimate means of moving from one distribution to another are specified by the principle of justice in transfer . . .' (p. 151). As far as I can see, he never explicitly identifies 'a just transfer' with 'a voluntary transfer', but he appears implicitly to equate the two. (b) His theory as I have formulated it obviously raises the prospect of an infinite regress. If distribution A arises out of distribution B by just means, we cannot tell whether A is just unless we know whether B is just; that will in turn depend on the justice of some previous distribution C, and so on. Nozick's answer would be that the regress is brought to an end by application of the principle of justice in acquisition. He is, however, disconcertingly vague about what constitutes a just original acquisition.

rights cannot be balanced against other goods, because it is not a good of that kind at all. Therefore, in particular, the pursuit of equality can never be justified if it involves the violation of rights.

The notion of rights as side-constraints, to be contrasted with goals, is an important one, but whether it can do all that Nozick requires of it is another matter. The fact still remains that different people's rights, even conceived in this way, may conflict, and may then have to be weighed against one another. Consider a society in which a large section of the population lives in abject poverty. To avoid starvation they have no alternative but to work in dangerous, degrading, and humiliating conditions from which their employers profit handsomely. The agreement to work in these conditions is at the superficial level a free contract, but the system which narrows people's choices in this drastic way is willingly maintained by those who benefit from it. I have previously, in chapters 2 and 3, mentioned mid-Victorian industrial Britain as an example, and there are plenty of other examples in the contemporary world. As I have noted in the earlier discussion of such cases, an obvious response to this situation would be to promote legislation which prohibited employers from employing people to work in such conditions, and this legislation would be backed by the threat of state coercion. Nozick would almost certainly regard such legislation as a violation of people's rights, coercively using them as a means to the betterment of others' condition. The obvious question is then: what about the rights of those who have to work in the appalling conditions? Are they not being denied the respect which is due to them as persons whose individuality is inviolable? And must we not, for the sake of their rights, be prepared to override to some extent the rights of those who are in a much more prosperous and more favoured position? It is at this point that Nozick would invoke the idea of rights as side-constraints rather than as goals. To weigh the rights of one group against those of another is, he thinks, to lapse into a 'utilitarianism of rights'. The rights-utilitarian takes the view that he should 'minimize the weighted amount of the violation of rights in the society, and that he should pursue this goal even through means that themselves violate people's rights' (p. 30). And this, according to Nozick, is a distortion of the very idea of rights.

Nozick's criticism of the idea of weighing rights against rights, or against other ethical considerations, is further developed in the following passage:

Side constraints express the inviolability of other persons. But why may not one violate persons for the greater social good? Individually, we each sometimes choose to undergo some pain or sacrifice for a greater benefit or to avoid a greater harm. . . . Why not, *similarly*, hold that some persons have to bear some costs that benefit other persons more, for the sake of the overall social good? But there is no *social entity* with a good that undergoes some sacrifice for its own good. There are only individual people, different individual people, with their own individual lives. Using one of these people for the benefit of others, uses him and benefits the others. Nothing more. What happens is that something is done to him for the sake of others. Talk of an overall social good covers this up. (Intentionally?) To use a person in this way does not sufficiently respect and take account of the fact that he is a separate person, that his is the only life he has. (pp. 32–3)

Again there seems to me to be an important point here. There is indeed a vital difference between an individual's sacrificing some things for his/her own good, and individuals being sacrificed for the sake of some supposed social good. In the former case, the individual is compensated by the long-term benefits for the sacrifices which he/she makes. In the latter case, if individuals are sacrificed, then for them there is no such compensation—the loss is absolute. But then we come up against the fact that, in cases like our example, someone *has* to be sacrificed. If the rights of the employers are treated as inviolable, then the oppressed are being sacrificed to the protecting of those rights—for them too the loss is absolute. There is no escaping the fact that rights conflict, freedoms conflict, the claims of some to be respected as persons whose individuality is inviolable conflict with the similar claims of others. In such conflicts, if A is not sacrificed to B, B will be sacrificed to A. The choice may seem an impossible one, but it is an inescapable one. Here it is important to remind ourselves that moral rights are not basic. If we think of them as fundamental ethical constraints, and if we think of them as purely negative limits, we may then be led to suppose that in any situation it is always possible to avoid violating anyone's rights, provided one does not actively and overtly coerce anyone. But, as I have argued, rights are not basic, they derive their importance from other more fundamental values such as the value of freedom, or the value of individual autonomy, or the need for respect. Consequently, rights may have to be overridden if they come into conflict with other ethical demands deriving from these same values. This does not mean a utilitarianism of rights; the objection to any utilitarian theory is precisely that, as a maximizing theory, it would justify sacrificing some people entirely if this would produce more good overall. What does follow is that if people's rights or freedoms conflict, some way has inescapably to be found of balancing them against one another, and the appropriate way of doing so is by appeal to the principle of equality, since that is precisely the principle which does not involve sacrificing some individuals for the sake of others.

The appeal to 'moral rights' does not, then, provide any additional support for the claim that the pursuit of equality threatens to destroy freedom. The concept of moral rights cannot itself establish that any particular set of freedoms has a special status, since it derives its ethical force from more fundamental concepts such as that of freedom. What about the concept of property rights, in particular? Does this add anything to the argument? It does, I think, introduce one important new point. Nozick emphasizes that any process by which material goods are produced is one which already, by its very nature, attaches those goods to particular owners. To that extent the goods are already distributed, and therefore to propose some view about the proper distribution of them, equal or otherwise, is to propose that they be *re*distributed, and thus to override the property rights of the existing owners. Nozick puts it like this:

To think that the task of a theory of distributive justice is to fill in the blank in "to each according to his—" is to be predisposed to search for a pattern; and the separate treatment of "from each according to his—" treats production and distribution as two separate and independent issues. On an entitlement view these are *not* two separate questions. ... The situation is *not* one of something's getting made, and there being an open question of who is to get it. Things come into the world already attached to people having entitlements over them. (pp. 159–60)

The link between production and distribution is something which I have previously discussed in chapter 6. There I took it to point to the conclusion that equality of power is more basic than equality of wealth. Nozick, however, sees it as strengthening his argument against an egalitarian principle or any other patterned principle of distributive justice. Why is this?

It is, I think, because Nozick implicitly assumes an individualistic model of production and ownership. We could formulate that model as follows:

*Model A.* Goods are produced by individuals, and they therefore come into the world attached to individuals. Any pattern of distribution, therefore, has to be imposed by some supra-individual agency, such as the state, which thus has to override the property rights of individuals in a coercive way.

To bring out the significance of this model, consider the contrast with two alternative models:

*Model B.* Goods are produced by individuals working for some corporate agency, such as a large privately-owned firm, and they therefore come into existence as the property of that corporate agency. A subsequent redistribution of the goods amongst the individuals who have produced them is therefore a way of countering the power of the corporate agency over those individuals.

*Model C.* Goods are produced communally by individuals working together as a group, and they therefore come into existence as the communal property of the group. The group then has to decide how the benefits are to be distributed amongst the individual members of the group.

I want to suggest that Nozick's assertion of the link between production and distribution introduces an important element of realism into the discussion. As he rightly says, goods do not just lie around waiting to be distributed, they are produced within a certain structure and a certain set of property-relations. The trouble is, however, that Nozick then loses sight of this realism. Model A, to which he implicitly appeals, bears little relation to the real world of production and ownership. The closest approximation to it would be a pre-industrial society of peasant proprietors, each owning their own plot of land and living on its products. The more probable cultural influence on Nozick is the historical experience of the American Frontier and of independent small farmers making a living for themselves by taking previously uncultivated land into individual ownership. Not even these are cases of purely individual production. The economic unit is still likely to be the family rather than the single individual, and individual proprietors are still likely to be dependent on exchange for at least some of their tools and implements, rather than being entirely self-sufficient. But at any rate it is this kind of economy which gives plausibility to the view that equality involves the redistribution of goods produced and owned by individuals. The fact is, however, that this is not the world in which we live. The contemporary real world of production and ownership has much more in common with Models B and C than with Model A. Likewise the kind of production and ownership-structure which egalitarians typically envisage is closer to B and C than to A. My reasons for making these claims are the following.

(i) In contemporary industrial societies the dominant form of ownership of the means of production is not individual ownership but corporate ownership. Though it may be true that in some sense corporate ownership is itself ultimately vested in individuals, the number of such individuals is relatively small in relation to the society as a whole, and a large proportion even of the nominal owners of a large company are shareholders who have very little in the way of effective rights of control over the affairs of the company. Most people do not own the goods which they produce or the means of producing them. For them the sphere of production is not one in which they have much scope for the exercise of individual freedom. The use of political power to redistribute material goods is thus not a restriction on their ownership rights as producers. And to the extent that this political power is exercised democratically, it may increase their freedom to control the products of their own activity.

(ii) More generally, the activity of production in modern industrial societies is at a deeper level a social rather than an individual activity. I have referred in chapter 4 to the fact that all economic activity depends upon a network of co-operative relations between individuals. This is true of any human society, but especially of large-scale modern societies with a complex division of labour. The product is a social product, created by the interacting activities of innumerable individuals organized in a systematic network of economic relations. This is true not just of the material goods which are produced but of the monetary income which is acquired by people engaged in the productive activity. Only in a superficial sense can it be said that any such wealth is created by the particular individual who acquires it. Consider now the following passage from Nozick's argument that redistributive taxation 'is on a par with forced labor' (p. 169):

[The] total product is produced by individuals laboring, using means of production others have saved to bring into existence, by people organizing production or creating means to produce new things or things in a new way. It is on this batch of individual activities that patterned distributional principles give each individual an enforceable claim. . . . Whether it is done through taxation on wages or on wages over a certain amount, or through seizure of profits, or through there being a big *social pot* so that it is not clear what's coming from where and what's going where, patterned principles of distributive justice involve appropriating the actions of other persons. Seizing results of someone's labor is equivalent to seizing hours from him and directing him to carry on various activities. This process whereby they take this decision from you makes them a *part-owner* of you; it gives them a property-right in you. (pp. 171–2)

Despite the incidental acknowledgement of a social dimension to economic activity (the 'social pot'), it is apparent that Nozick thinks of the economic product as something produced primarily by individuals, and the redistribution as emanating from a source entirely external to those same individuals. Taxation he regards as 'on a par with forced

labour' because 'they' are taking from 'you' the results of
'your' labour. In fact, however, these results are the results of
the labour of countless individuals, and the apportioning of
these results among the individuals in the form of wages,
profits, etc. is simply a matter of the particular conventions
within which those individuals happen to be operating. These
conventions may be ones which have been created by the
voluntary contracts into which people have entered; but then
the same may be true of the further arrangements such as
taxation and its use to finance various kinds of social services.
The wage-relation is no more sacrosanct than taxation as a
way of apportioning the products of people's combined
labours. In so far as Nozick supposes otherwise, he places
himself within the tradition of those who have ascribed to the
labour-contract a quite unjustifiably unique status as the
embodiment of individual freedom.

(iii) In making points (i) and (ii) I have gone along with
Nozick's assumption that patterned principles will redistribute
the property of individuals, and have been concerned to show
that the goods owned by individuals are, in a deeper sense, a
social product. Lastly, however, we have to remind ourselves
that patterned principles do not have to work in that
*re*distributive way. If we are impressed, as Nozick is, with the
link between distribution and production, we may conclude
not that the search for a particular pattern of distribution
must be abandoned as coercive, but that the desired pattern
of distribution must be a pattern embedded in the process of
production itself. This is why thoroughgoing egalitarians
have argued not just for an egalitarian distribution of
material goods, but for the common ownership of the means
of production. If the means of production are communally
owned and controlled (genuinely and not just nominally so),
then the process of distribution ceases to be a matter of
reappropriating the property of individuals, and becomes a
matter of communally assigning the uses of the communal
product. The point is, once again, that equality in respect of
material wealth must rest on a basis of equality in respect of
power. This is the idea which Nozick, in the passage quoted
above, caricatures as the idea of a 'social pot'. Trapped as he
is within his individualistic assumptions, he still seems to

think in terms of individuals being forced to put their individual property into the social pot. He ignores the possibility that what goes into the pot may be, from the start, socially produced and socially owned.

The possibility is briefly acknowledged in another passage, where Nozick argues that even in a socially-owned economy individuals would engage in voluntary transfers which would upset the pattern of social ownership.

I melt down some of my personal possessions ... and build a machine out of the material. I offer you, and others, a philosophy lecture once a week in exchange for your cranking the handle on my machine whose products I exchange for yet other things, and so on. . . . Each person might participate to gain things over and above their allotment. . . . Private property even in means of production would occur in a socialist society that did not forbid people to use as they wished some of the resources they are given under the socialist distribution. . . . The socialist society would have to forbid capitalist acts between consenting adults. (pp. 162–3)

Here I would want to invoke my earlier distinction between the structural features of a society and what goes on in the interstices of the structure, and my suggestion that egalitarianism is more concerned with the former than with the latter. The dividing line between the two cannot be drawn with any precision, but it is clear that an egalitarian social policy would not be intended to regulate every minor exchange of favours. The point at which such exchanges start to become relevant would be the point at which they start to give some people a significant degree of established power over others. To take Nozick's example, there is a crucial difference between my arranging for people to take an occasional turn at cranking the handle on my machine, and my employing a regular workforce over whose activities I thereby exercise a degree of control. The latter situation would be the proper concern of an egalitarian policy; but here my point (i) applies, that overriding people's property rights may be justified if those property rights give them power over others and thus restrict the freedom of others.[9]

I conclude that neither the concept of moral rights in general, nor that of property rights in particular, gives any additional support to the anti-egalitarian argument. Conflicting freedoms have inescapably to be weighed against one another, and that weighing cannot be blocked simply by christening a particular set of freedoms as 'rights'. In particular, property rights may be outweighed if they are themselves a source of power and of control over the freedoms of others. The central thrust of an egalitarian policy, however, will be not the overriding of individual property rights but the establishing of a communal ownership and control of those institutions which constitute the basic structure of a society. To do this will be to found equality of wealth on equality of power.

Throughout this chapter, then, we have been reminded that our defence of equality must treat equality of power as the fundamental aspect of equality. The ideals of freedom and equality converge upon the ideal of equality of power. In the final chapter we must return to that idea and must at last confront the question: is equality of power a real possibility?

Singer's 'Rights and the Market' is another excellent discussion of Nozick and rights. Cohen's article is one of several which he has written on this theme. Others include 'Freedom, Justice and Capitalism' in *New Left Review* 126 (1981); 'Nozick on Appropriation' in *New Left Review* 150 (1985); and 'Self-Ownership, World Ownership, and Equality: Part II' in *Social Philosophy and Policy* vol. 3 (1986). Together they add up to a detailed rebuttal of the so-called 'libertarian' critique of equality.

# 8

## Equality of Power: Some
## Utopian Speculations

THE argument which has emerged from the preceding chapters is that the ideals of freedom and of equality converge upon the idea of equality of power. If freedom and equality are to prove in practice complementary rather than conflicting ideals, they must do so through the medium of social institutions which enable everyone to share equally in the power to control the activities of their own society. To complete the argument it therefore becomes necessary to show that equality of power is indeed a real possibility, by indicating in a plausible way the form which such institutions might take. I have said something about this, in general terms, in chapter 6, but need to say more, at a more detailed and more practical level. This does not mean offering a programme of political reforms or a set of blueprints for the future. It does mean describing possible institutions in sufficient detail to render convincing the claim that those institutions could operate in practice and could be compatible with what we know of human psychology and social behaviour. As I indicated in chapter 1, a coherent logical analysis of concepts does not take us very far if those concepts can have no application to the real world.

Some would say that the concept of 'equality of power' is open to criticism on just those grounds. J. R. Lucas, for instance, writes as follows:

If men, as we now know them, are to co-exist in civil society there must be sanctions: this follows from the fact that some people are bloody-minded, and will do violence to others unless restrained by force or the threat of force. Civil society is, therefore, dependent on there being certain people in a position to coerce others, people, that is, with power. Power cannot be equally divided and distributed over the whole population. It is necessarily concentrated in few hands.[1]

[1] J. R. Lucas, 'Against Equality', in *Philosophy*, vol. 40 (1965), pp. 303–4, and reprinted in H. A. Bedau (ed.) *Justice and Equality*, p. 147.

This argument derives its plausibility from the fact that particular instances of the exercise of power take the form of some people (a limited group) wielding power over other people. One might even agree that this follows from the very nature of power. However, when particular people exercise power on particular occasions in this way, they normally do so as agents of a more generally shared authority. A typical example of the kind which Lucas has in mind would be the exercise of power by the police in apprehending a criminal; but of course there is more to the situation than that, and the power which is exercised here is not normally a power which belongs simply and solely to the police, it derives from a complex structure of authority. The question then is whether the more general sharing of power which lies behind these overt manifestations can amount to anything like an equal sharing. If that is to be possible, it must be in virtue of democratic institutions, and it is therefore in this direction that we must look.[2]

It can scarcely be maintained that existing democratic institutions achieve a real equality of power. Certainly they ensure that power is shared, and if they work properly they ensure that everyone has a share in power, but they do not ensure that everyone has an equal share. Most people's institutionalized power is limited to voting in elections. The leaders who are thereby elected exercise a very much greater power than those who merely elect them. This is one major and obvious inequality. The other main respect in which existing democratic systems fail to achieve equality of power is that there are whole areas of our life, and especially of our economic life, where power is exercised by decision-makers who are not elected at all, and are in no way answerable to ordinary people.

The obvious response is then to suggest that democracy, if it is to approximate more closely to the equal sharing of

---

[2] For the discussion of democracy which occupies the remainder of this chapter, I have found the following particularly helpful: Robert A. Dahl, *After the Revolution?* (New Haven 1970); Carole Pateman, *Participation and Democratic Theory* (Cambridge 1970); C. B. Macpherson, *The Life and Times of Liberal Democracy* (Oxford 1977); and John Burnheim, 'Statistical Democracy' in *Radical Philosophy* 27 (1981).

power, must be extended in two corresponding respects. First, we need a greater degree of 'direct' or 'participatory' democracy, rather than mere 'representative' democracy, so that ordinary people can directly exercise power themselves rather than simply elect others to exercise it on their behalf. Second, we need to bring more areas of social life, and especially economic life, under democratic control.These are the kinds of changes which have regularly been proposed by the advocates of radical democracy. The aim is to enable ordinary people to exercise direct control over their own activities as the producers and consumers of goods and services, through institutions such as citizens' assemblies controlling the activities of the local community, and workers' councils controlling the activities of the workplace.

However, if this is the obvious response, the difficulties are equally obvious. There are practical difficulties of size, and of time. Direct democracy, understood as the participation of everyone in the making of decisions, would seem to be unworkable on anything other than the smallest scale. It might just be possible for all the workers in a very small economic enterprise, or all the adult inhabitants of a small village or neighbourhood, to attend a meeting where issues can be debated and decisions made. For any larger unit it must surely be impossible. The affairs of a large modern city, let alone a modern nation-state or a multi-national business enterprise, could not conceivably be dealt with in such a fashion.

Even at the small-scale level where direct democracy could cope with the constraints of size, the constraints of time would still militate against equal participation in decision-making. Most people do not have enough time to be constantly involved in running the affairs of their own community or their own workplace. Many are likely to have to spend a good deal of their time working. Modern technology could no doubt, if properly applied, reduce working hours, but there are limits to the amount of time which can be set free by these means, and in any case a majority of people would probably prefer to devote most of their non-working hours to other, more attractive pursuits. Moreover, even within a mass meeting such as that of a citizens' assembly or a workers' council, the constraints of time will operate in further ways. In a meeting of hundreds or even thousands of people, not everyone can participate on equal terms. Everyone can have a vote on the final decision, but only a relatively few people can speak. The active formulating of policies is therefore likely to be done mainly by a minority who are particularly well-informed, or quick-thinking, or self-confident, or persuasive speakers. Thus the possibility of equality of power seems to recede again.

To these practical difficulties of direct democracy may be added further objections, reasons for thinking it to be not only impractical but also undesirable. Two objections in particular I want to dwell on. The first may be called the problem of human limitations, and it is the problem which has always most concerned the critics of democracy, from Plato onwards. In part it is the problem of competence. The making of decisions about the affairs of a community or an economic enterprise requires expert knowledge—of town planning, or of architecture, or of economics, or of the technical processes of production—and most people simply do not have that kind of technical expertise. So far, however, these are limitations which can be accommodated within a functioning democratic system. Ordinary people can listen to the advice of experts, but retain for themselves the power to make decisions in the light of that advice. Moreover, the experience of doing this is itself an educative process (a point stressed in the classic justificatory theories of democracy). The lay person can, over time and by 'learning on the job', develop the ability to assess the advice of experts, both by becoming better informed about the subject-matter of their expertise and by developing more general powers of judgement and discrimination. The real problems of human limitations are not the problems of lay people's limited expertise, but more deeply rooted psychological limitations. Notoriously, people can be manipulated by appeals to their emotions. The ambitious and unscrupulous politician who has a flair for engaging in such manipulation can all too easily induce people to make decisions which are rash, biased, superficial, or irrational. Plato, in *The Republic*, describes how ordinary people, when they are given political power, crowd into the seats in the assembly . . . and, with a great deal of noise and a great lack of moderation, shout and clap their approval or disapproval of whatever is proposed or done, till the rocks and the whole place re-echo, and redouble the noise of their boos and applause. Can a young man remain unmoved by all this? How can his individual training stand the strain? Won't he be swamped by the flood of popular praise and blame, and carried away before it till he finds himself agreeing with popular ideas of right and wrong, behaving like the crowd and becoming one of them?[3]

Political leaders are thus led to cultivate the art of pandering to people's superficial desires and emotions, rather than looking to the true good of the community.

Suppose a man was in charge of a large and powerful animal, and made a study of its moods and wants; he would learn when to approach and handle it, when and why it was especially savage or gentle, what the different noises it made meant, and what tone of voice to use to soothe or annoy it. All this he might learn by long experience and familiarity, and then call it a science, and reduce it to a system and set up to teach it. But he would not really know which of the creature's tastes and desires was fair or unfair, good or bad, right or wrong; he would simply use the terms on the basis of its reactions, calling what pleased it good, what annoyed it bad. . . . But is there really any difference between him and the man who thinks that the knowledge of the passions and pleasures of the mass of the common people is a science . . . ?[4]

In the modern world we may feel that nothing has changed except that the techniques of persuasion and manipulation have become more sophisticated, and the media of mass communication have enabled them to be employed on a vastly greater scale. Anyone who was in Britain at the time of the Falklands War must acknowledge the frightening capacity of political leaders to whip up popular emotion, and the strength of the temptation for them to do so for the sake of political expediency. Plato's response to this problem was to distinguish between the majority of human beings who are ruled by their emotions and the small minority who are ruled by their reason, and to insist that in a just society political

[3] Plato, *The Republic* 492B–C. I have quoted from H. D. P. Lee's translation in the Penguin Classics series.
[4] Ibid. 493A–D.

power should be exercised solely by the latter group. Without necessarily going as far as Plato one may feel that in the light of these human limitations the equal sharing of political power is hardly desirable.

The second reason for thinking that the democratic sharing of power may be undesirable is what I have previously referred to as the problem of the tyranny of the majority. As I mentioned at the beginning of chapter 2, it is a problem to which Mill is particularly sensitive, and it is a problem which is especially relevant to our present consideration of the relations between democracy, equality, and freedom. A system of majority voting makes it possible for the majority to dominate the minority as tyrannically as any autocrat. This will be particularly so if certain people are permanently or regularly in the minority. Though formally they have the same share in power as everyone else, they have no real control over what is decided, and their votes thus count for nothing. It may, therefore, seem that if equality of power is identified with a system of radically democratic decision-making, it is bound to destroy the freedom of those who are consistently out-voted.

Our fundamental problem thus reasserts itself. If may be that, at the purely theoretical level, the values of freedom and equality are consistent or even complementary, but this is small comfort if, at the level of concrete and workable institutions, they come into conflict and pose an inescapable choice between institutions which promote freedom and those which promote equality. The questions which we have to take up now are thus essentially practical ones, questions about whether we can devise institutions which will effectively embody the values of both freedom and equality. It is not a philosophical task to show in detail how this can be done. Nevertheless, our philosophical enterprise will turn out to be an empty one unless we can plausibly indicate at least the possibility of resolving these practical difficulties, and can describe in general terms the kinds of institutions which would be needed.

I shall now consider, in turn, a number of institutional forms, and ask how far each might help to resolve in practice the four problems which we have posed: the problems of size and of time, the problem of human limitations, and the problem of the tyranny of the majority.

*Small-group Democracy* offers a possible way of dealing with the third and fourth problems. There are important differences between the way in which decisions are made in a large meeting or assembly and the way in which they can be made in a small group (by 'small' I mean about twenty at most, and ideally less than a dozen). In a large meeting most people are bound to be mainly passive participants, listening to the arguments and then casting their votes. The debate is usually conducted in terms of set positions, proposing and opposing a resolution. As anyone knows who has taken part in such debates, the business of proposing amendments in an attempt to change the terms of the discussion is typically a difficult and frustrating one. At the end of the day those who have been outvoted, and perhaps also many of those who voted for the successful proposal, will feel dissatisfied with the outcome, will feel that important points have not been taken into account and that the successful proposal has not been formulated in such a way as to take adequate account of all the issues.

By contrast, small-group decision-making does at least offer the possibility of a different mode of proceeding. It provides no guarantees; as we know, committee meetings can be as frustrating as any larger meeting. Nevertheless there is at least the possibility for everyone to participate actively rather than be simply the recipients of other people's oratorical skills. It is possible for proposals to be reformulated, and for new ideas to emerge, in the search for a consensus which will take account of everyone's views. The discussion does not have to be confined to arguments for or against a given proposal; it can change course, a new approach can be tried, proposals can be withdrawn and the issues redefined. It may then be possible to reach a decision by consensus without taking a vote, and therefore without leaving some people in an outvoted minority. Everyone can see the decision as, in a real sense, *their* decision, even if it is not what they would ideally have wanted. If a vote does have to be taken, those who are out-voted may at least be able to feel that they have had their say, and have not just been ignored. Along these lines, then, there may be some prospect of overcoming the problem of the tyranny of the majority.

Small-group decision-making also seems to offer a better chance of tackling the problem of human limitations, since it has a better chance of being a relatively rational process. There is less scope for manipulative rhetoric. Inevitably some people are more eloquent and more persuasive than others, but in a small group they can more easily be challenged, questioned, forced to explain more clearly what they mean, instead of being allowed to take refuge in impressive-sounding but evasive phrases. Participation in such decision-making also has more chance of being an educative process, because people are likely to be more actively involved; they are forced to think more for themselves rather than be content to sit back and let themselves be persuaded.

Unfortunately, though small-group democracy may offer some prospect of solving our second pair of problems, it does so at the cost of making the first pair insurmountable. To maximize the possibilities of rational discussion and the reaching of a consensus, the optimum size for a meeting would be about ten people. A meeting of a hundred people would be much less satisfactory, and a mass meeting of a thousand would almost entirely have lost the advantages of small-group democracy. Open-ended discussion would be bound to give way to a set-piece debate. How, we must then ask, could any large institution or community, let alone a society the size of a modern nation-state, be run by a system of small-group democracy? There seems to be a direct conflict here: on the one hand, the more democratic a system is to be, the more people it must involve in its procedures; on the other hand, the more it tries to tackle the problem of human limitations and the problem of the tyranny of the majority, the smaller the number of people it can involve. The problem of time seems equally inexorable. Open-ended discussion, allowing for the introduction of new suggestions and working through to a consensus, is by its very nature time-consuming. Full-time decision-makers may be able to afford it, but it is difficult to see how everyone could help to run the affairs of their community in this way.

*Referendum Democracy* is an option at the opposite pole from small-group democracy, and with the reverse set of advantages and disadvantages. It copes with the first pair of problems, but has nothing to offer to the solution of the second pair. Issues which can be simply formulated, so as to admit of a 'Yes' or 'No' answer, can be decided by a large-scale referendum, and, with modern methods of communication, there is no limit to the number of people who can participate in such a decision. Time can hardly be a problem; a good deal of time may be demanded from those who have to organize and administer a referendum, but the casting of a vote, which is all that is demanded of most of those who take part, is the matter of a moment. That, however, is of course precisely the weakness of a referendum. The act of decision-making is divorced from the process of discussion. There may be some kind of debate leading up to the referendum. Interested parties may campaign for a 'Yes' or 'No' vote, and the issues may be discussed through the press and radio and television. The vast majority of voters, however, cannot possibly participate in this debate. At best they will be passive viewers and listeners, at worst they will completely ignore it. A great many of them are likely to cast their votes in ignorance, on the basis of prejudice or in response to the emotive manipulation of attitudes. Participation in a referendum can be an educative experience for those who choose to make it so, but there is no pressure on people to learn from it. They are not challenged to articulate their views and defend them, they need only vote. This separation of decision from disccussion exacerbates also the problem of the tyranny of the majority. The terms of the decision cannot be accommodated to any new views or suggestions which might emerge in the course of the debate. The issue has to be simply formulated in advance, and because the answer has to be 'Yes' or 'No', a referendum is paradigmatically the form of decision-making which polarizes people into a successful majority and a defeated minority.

Given that small-group democracy and referendum democracy have contrasting advantages and disadvantages, we now have to ask whether there is any way of combining mass participation with the advantages of small-group decision-making.

*Decentralization* is one possible answer. The aim here would be to have decisions made as far as possible at a local rather than a national level, the general principle being that issues should be decided by those who are directly and mainly affected by them. The preferred decision-making units would be the workplace, the town, or the neighbourhood. These, however, are not themselves units which are small enough for small-group democracy as I have described it. Decentralization combined with direct democracy would require the politics of the mass meeting rather than the small group. This would at least have the advantage of offering the opportunity for more active participation by ordinary people than referendum democracy, and would thus encourage the existence of a more educated and informed populace; but the problems of demagogy and of majority rule would remain. When Plato and his contemporaries originally identified those problems, they found them precisely in the politics of the mass meeting, exemplified by the behaviour of the assembly in the Athenian city-state.

Decentralization itself also has its own particular difficulties. A great many matters simply cannot be dealt with at the local level; or, if they are, they can be dealt with only in an inadequate and partial way. This may be true even if they are primarily local issues. Consider such examples as the following: a firm is in danger of collapsing because its supply of components has been disrupted, or because the state of the roads or the closing of a railway makes it difficult to transport the products to where they are sold; the survival of a village is threatened because work is no longer available in the next town, or because the villagers can no longer travel to work as a result of the withdrawal of a bus service; a river running through the middle of a town is being polluted by a factory upstream in the next district. These are all matters of direct local concern, but they cannot be adequately dealt with by decisions at the level of the workplace or the village or the town. For all the desirability of small-scale democracy, many local issues are at the same time inescapably large-scale issues. Can we then find any way of linking the different levels? Is there any way of bringing small-group or local democracy to bear on large-scale issues?

*Pyramidal Democracy* has sometimes been proposed as an answer. Such a scheme is explicitly intended to deal with the problem of linking the different levels of decision-making. What is envisaged is a system with a number of tiers; for the sake of illustration let us imagine a four-tier system operating at the level of the neighbourhood or locality, the city or county, the region, and the national level. (We could also imagine an analogous structure for running the affairs of an industry or service, with the lowest tier being that of the local workplace, such as a factory, school, hospital etc.). Issues are discussed at the local level in some kind of assembly or mass meeting. Some of them can be dealt with entirely at that level. Those which require wider consideration will be forwarded to a meeting at the next level, where the presentation of them will be entrusted to an elected delegate. All such delegates are mandated, accountable, and recallable. That is to say, before each meeting they are told by their electors how they should vote; after each meeting they must report back about how they voted, and, in particular, if they have voted other than in accordance with their mandate they must give their reasons for doing so; and they can be replaced at any time by another delegate if the electors feel that they are not being properly represented. Just as the neighbourhood meeting will pass matters on to the city meeting through its elected delegate, so likewise the city meeting will have its delegate at the regional meeting, and the regional meeting will have its delegate in the national assembly. Similarly, matters which are initiated at one of the higher levels will be passed down to the local level for the local delegate to be mandated, the local delegates will vote at the city meeting to mandate their delegate to the region, and so on, back up the pyramid.

The attraction of such a system is that, unlike referendum democracy, it seems to provide a way for ordinary people to participate actively in the process of discussion and debate; and it allows such decision-making to deal with larger issues which are not amenable to decentralization. The key to the operation of such a system is the practice of mandating. This is what gives it its advantages, but mandating has its own drawbacks. Such a system may allow for discussion and debate at the initial, local level, but if at all the higher levels decisions have to be made by meetings consisting entirely of mandated delegates, there would seem to be no room left for further discussion to affect the outcome. There might, in a formal sense, be a debate in which the delegates can state the arguments for the positions which they are mandated to support; but if they then all vote according to their mandate, the resulting decision cannot be said to be the outcome of this debate. Rather, it would be the product of a purely mechanical process of voting, to which the debate was irrelevant. Indeed, this being so, one might as well make the process literally a mechanical one. Decisions on matters at any level higher than the local level could be arrived at simply by counting the votes from all the local meetings, and there would be no need for further meetings or for delegates. Looked at in this way, such a system merges into referendum democracy, and indeed it might best be regarded as a more desirable way of conducting referenda, helping to ensure that the voting in the referendum is preceded by a full debate.

These drawbacks to pyramidal democracy assume the operation of strict mandating. Of course it does not have to be like that. Mandating can be flexible. Delegates can be given, by those who mandate them, a general idea of how they should vote, but can also be allowed scope to decide differently if the subsequent debate introduces new considerations and arguments which the delegate regards as convincing. That, indeed, is the point of saying that delegates should be not only mandated but also accountable. It is assumed that delegates will sometimes depart from their mandate, and that they should then give an account of why they did so. The more flexible the mandating is, the more we move away from pure direct democracy to the more familiar institutions of representational democracy. There are in fact reasons for thinking that there would always be strong pressure towards a representational system, one in which elected representatives have to engage in independent decision-making, because of considerations which constitute further difficulties for pyramidal democracy. The decisions made at the higher levels of the pyramid have to add up to a coherent policy for the city, the region, the country, the international community, and so on. The formulation of coherent policies cannot be simply a mechanical process, a mere adding together of decisions produced by the mandated votes of delegates. Take the case of developing a coherent national policy to tackle the problem of unemployment. This is likely to involve decisions about what kinds of investment in new industries should be encouraged in different parts of the country. This will then run up against the decisions of local communities who do not want this or that industrial development in their own area. Either the national policy is allowed to ride roughshod over the local preferences, in which case the extent of direct democracy shrinks rapidly, or the individual views of local communities are given serious consideration, in which case the overall plan has to be modified every time a local objection is upheld. Moreover, quite apart from the question of the local impact, the local community meetings will each have their own views about the overall national policy. Each may propose its own modifications and amendments, and strict direct democracy would require that all of these should then be referred to all the other local community meetings for consideration. The process would be almost interminable, and it is very difficult to see how any coherent policy could emerge from it. In the light of these considerations it is clear that strict mandating would be quite unworkable. The mandating would have to be flexible and delegates would have to be given a considerable degree of autonomy to work out policies at the higher levels. The trouble is then that the mandating would tend to become more and more nominal. Real power would gravitate away from the local meetings to the delegates, who would simply have to report back to their electors periodically—perhaps every year, perhaps every four or five years, since coherent policies have to be developed over a period, and given time in which to work. This very quickly begins to look like the system of representational democracy with which we are familiar and of which I have said that, whatever its merits, it hardly amounts to equality of power. I do not say that the pressures in this direction are bound to be irresistible. There is, I think, considerable scope for the operation of pyramidal democracy as a way of involving everyone in the discussion of at least the broad lines of national policies. But the pressures limiting this involvement will be strong, and will always tend to encourage the re-emergence of professional politicians with a virtual monopoly of power. Further ways are therefore needed of promoting the active involvement of ordinary people in decision-making at anything other than the most local level.

*The Jury System*   seems to me to be one other possibility worth considering at this point. At present we do not ordinarily think of it as a political institution. Nevertheless I can see no reason why the use of such a system should not be extended from the legal to the political sphere. Its essential principle is that a group of a dozen people chosen at random is capable of listening to a quantity of evidence submitted to it, of deliberating together and arriving at a judgement of that evidence, and the principle seems to me to be equally applicable to at least some kinds of political decision-making. It was a principle central to the operation of ancient Athenian democracy, where council members and many of the officials were chosen by lot. If the principle of choosing people by lot is combined with the principle of rotation, so that the members of a political 'jury', like those of a legal jury, serve only for a short period of time and are then not called on for a number of years, we then have a way of dealing with the problems of size and of time. Decisions can be made by ordinary citizens rather than by full-time officials or elected politicians, but since they take it in turns to perform this role rather than all doing it at once, they do not have to do it in a mass meeting or a national referendum. For as long as a person's turn lasted, it would be time-consuming (and arrangements would have to be made for paid absence from work, as with the present legal jury system), but since it would not last for long, everyone would have time to take a turn. What the jury system then offers are the very great advantages of small-group democracy, which I described above; decisions can be the outcome of a process of discussion, and it is possible to work towards agreement rather than mechanically voting in a way which divides people into a majority and a minority. Bear in mind that this is precisely the way in which a legal jury is required to operate. When the jury retires, it has to organize itself and conduct its own discussion, and the object of the discussion is to arrive at unanimity or, failing that, at near-unanimity.

For all these reasons the existing jury system is one of the most democratic of institutions, and its extension to the political sphere could radically increase the active involvement of ordinary people in decision-making. It would help to take power out of the hands of full-time politicians and officials. The latter could advise, inform, and advocate, as the judge and the prosecution and defence counsel do in relation to a legal jury, but the actual decisions could be made by ordinary people selected at random.

As I acknowledged earlier in this chapter, there are obviously limits to most people's expertise. It would be difficult to maintain plausibly that a dozen citizens selected at random could then be given the task of running the country (though one does sometimes wonder whether they might not make a better job of it). People's competence may grow with experience, but since, as I have said, the essence of the 'jury' idea is that people take it in turns and serve only for a short time, the system still needs experts who, through long experience and training, have acquired the necessary knowledge and skills. The function of a 'jury' has to be to keep a check on the experts, and sometimes to adjudicate when the experts disagree. There is ample scope for this. I will mention two examples where this role is not at present, but could perfectly well be, performed by a 'jury'. Take the case of a public inquiry, of the kind which is regularly set up to look into controversial matters such as the siting of a new road or reservoir, an airport or a power station, or the construction of a shopping complex, or a multi-storey car park. An appointed inspector listens to the views of a large number of interested groups and individuals, receives the conflicting advice of experts, and then arrives at a judgement. There is no reason why this role could not be performed by a 'jury' of people chosen by lot, and such a system could be used much more extensively than it is at present. As a second example, consider the fairly recent introduction of the system of 'select committees' in Parliament—small committees charged with looking into a particular area of decision-making, who call ministers and civil servants to appear before them, listen to their evidence, and then form an assessment of a particular set of policies or decisions. The operative assumption here is that the members of the committee are not themselves experts, but can assess the evidence of experts. Again it seems to me that if this role can be performed by MPs, it can also be performed by 'juries' chosen by lot—perhaps at the national level, and still more at the local level.

A 'jury' system, then, still needs experts and professional politicians. What it provides is a way of making them more accountable. As such it can supplement pyramidal democracy and referendum democracy; it provides an alternative means whereby policies which cannot be decentralized can nevertheless be referred back to ordinary people for their assessment. Unlike pyramidal democracy and referendum democracy, it is a way of combining this with the advantages of small-group discussion. But, like them, it runs up against the problem that full-time decision-makers have to develop coherent long-term policies, and that this inevitably limits their accountability.

I have now reviewed five possible ways of extending democracy and thereby working towards a more equal sharing of power: small-group democracy, referendum democracy, decentralization, pyramidal democracy, and the jury system. It is clear from the review that no one of these is a panacea. Each has its difficulties. What we can do now, however, is to consider how these various options might effectively complement each other, and might together add up to a system more democratic than anything with which we are currently familiar.

There are undoubted limits to the possibilities of decentralization. Nevertheless, within those limits, effective democracy must surely mean that decision-making has to be decentralized as much as possible. There are hard choices to be made here. In particular, as we have previously noted, there are hard choices to be made from the standpoint of equality. It may well be the case that certain kinds of material inequality have to be accepted for the sake of the greater equality of power which could be made possible by economic decentralization.

Decentralization means that matters which primarily affect the local community or the local workplace are decided at that level. There remains the question of how they can be decided more democratically. What is needed here is some combination of small-group democracy, mass meetings, and the accountability of politicians and managers and officials. Even at this local level, effective decision-making requires full-time decision-makers, but they do not have to decide everything and their decisions do not have to go unchallenged. The broad lines of policy can periodically be referred to mass meetings of citizens or workers, and policy details can to some extent be assessed by representative smaller groups. I would suggest that the jury system is particularly appropriate here, where there are fewer limitations on people's competence. At this local level, ordinary people have more direct experience of the issues, and can effectively assess the proposals of politicians and managers.

At the higher levels, regional and national and international, the possibilities for greater democracy must reside in the increased use of referenda, and the greater accountability of full-time decision-makers. We have seen that there are limits to both these possibilities, but within those limits a good deal could be done. It is perfectly possible to hold referenda occasionally on contentious issues of basic principle. We have seen that one disadvantage of referenda is that they allow people to vote in an irresponsible way, without any real consideration of the issues; but we have also noted that an alternative way of conducting referenda is for the voting to be done in local meetings, after a discussion. Referendum democracy then begins to coincide with a limited form of pyramidal democracy. Inevitably, I think, referenda are bound to be confined to matters of very general basic policy, but across a wider range of issues full-time decision-makers, such as elected politicians, can be required to be regularly answerable to the people they represent—for example, to occasional mass meetings of their constituents and to more frequent 'juries' chosen by lot from among their constituents.

We should also note that in the economic sphere even the practice of election has made little headway as yet. Managers and directors of economic enterprises are not normally elected by those whose activities they manage and direct, in the way that politicians are, but they could be and ought to be, and this would be an important extension of democracy.

We have seen that the holding of referenda, and the attempt to make elected decision-makers more accountable, are both open to the problem of human limitations. Ordinary people can be manipulated, by the politicians and officials themselves and by other people who have control of powerful and persuasive means of communication. This, however, is where the different kinds of democracy can complement each other. The more experience people have, at the local level, of assessing and criticizing their full-time officials, the greater will be their competence and their capacity for independent judgement when it comes to larger-scale issues. The experience of democracy, at every level, is itself the best education for democracy.

Although I have acknowledged their limits, these ideas may nevertheless seem wildly utopian. I have in fact called them 'utopian speculations', but I want in conclusion to consider how far that description is appropriate. In one obvious sense they are indeed utopian. They are ideals rather than realities—what ought to be rather than what is. I have described possible institutions which at present exist only to a limited degree, and I have argued that if they existed more extensively they would make for greater freedom and greater equality.

However, the term 'utopian' also suggests ideas which are unrealistic, which not only do not but could not apply to the real world, and in that sense I want to resist the appellation. The institutions which I have sketched are not unrealistic in the way in which I have suggested, for instance, that Nozick's theories are. Nozick and other writers of the individualistic libertarian school presuppose a world which is entirely remote from anything we can recognize, a world in which the means of production, in particular, are owned by individuals rather than by corporate bodies. By contrast, the forms of democratic decision-making which I have considered are ones which could function within the social world which we know. They are extensions of forms with which we are familiar. There is nothing utopian in itself about small-group decision-making, and the problem there is how to link it with other institutions so as to give it a democratic character. Referenda and the jury system are institutions which already operate in societies such as our own, and my suggestion is that they could operate more extensively. The decentralization of decision-making is a matter of degree; some matters are decentralized, and more of them could be. The least familiar of the democratic forms which I have described is pyramidal democracy but, though this is not at present an accepted feature of the political system, many non-governmental organizations administer themselves in this way. We know, therefore, that it is a form of decision-making which can operate in large-scale modern societies. All of these, then, are genuine possibilities. If I had envisaged, say, the wholesale transfer of ancient Athenian democracy to the modern nation-state, that would indeed have been utopian in a derogatory sense, but that is not what I have been doing.

The institutions which I have described *could* operate in the world which we know. But at what cost? Some would say that the cost is too great, and it is at this point that the accusation of being unrealistic becomes more difficult to meet. I have talked about the time-consuming nature of radical democracy, and the problem of shortcomings in people's judgement and understanding. It may be that these problems could be overcome to the extent of making radical democracy operable, but would they nevertheless involve a sacrifice of efficiency, and would this be too great a price to bear?

There is no simple answer to these questions, but the first thing to be said is that efficiency can be measured in different ways. There are egalitarian and non-egalitarian conceptions of efficiency, and from an egalitarian point of view the efficiency of a system is to be assessed not by asking 'Would any alternative system make some people better off?' but by asking 'Would any alternative system improve the condition of the least well-off?' That is the substance of Rawls's difference principle. I have said something about it in previous chapters, and have acknowledged that it might justify some departures from equality in respect of material goods. I also said, however, that it cannot be the appropriate principle to determine the distribution of power, since inequalities of power necessarily could not increase the power of the least powerful. Now my reason for discussing radical democracy has, of course, been to show in concrete terms what equality of power might amount to. So even if radical democracy turned out to be less efficient in promoting the material prosperity of the least well-off, we should have to set against that loss the distinctive gains of equality of power—the goods of co-operative relations between people and the opportunities for people to control their own lives and employ to the full their distinctively human capacities for discriminative choice and judgement.

Now, of course, we cannot be cavalier about material prosperity. Those non-material goods might have to be sacrificed if radical democracy led to economic disaster. Would it do so? We do not know for certain that it would not, and we could only find out by experience. As I have already indicated in chapter 6, my own expectation would be that the extension of democracy would increase people's commitment to their working activity, would draw on a wider range of skills and initiative, and would thereby make for greater efficiency. That expectation, however, could be tested only by extending democracy and observing the consequences. Again, therefore, it is important that the 'utopian' institutions which I have described are not totally remote from existing practices but an extension of them; the introduction of them can be a matter of degree, and the process can be one of trial and error.

There remains one other interpretation which could be given to the charge of utopianism, and it is the one which I would most strenuously repudiate. To engage in utopian thinking is, it may be said, to erect a set of abstract ideals which are simply the product of a priori theorizing and bear no relation to what human beings actually want or need. My aim in this book has been precisely to show that freedom and equality are not abstract ideals in that sense. They are values grounded in experience. We value freedom because we find fulfilment in the directing of our own lives, thinking for ourselves, and making choices for ourselves. We value equality because we join with one another in relations of co-operation, and those relations carry with them a commitment to treat one another as equals. The two values come together in the experience of a co-operative community in which people run their own lives not just individually but collectively, through the processes of democracy. My description of radical democracy is thus an attempt to articulate a form of life in which the convergence of freedom and equality would not just have the status of a philosophical thesis, but would be directly experienced. How fully that possibility can be realized remains to be seen.

# Index

animals 96 n.
apartheid 93–4
Aristotle 10, 18
Arthur, J. 58 n.

Bakunin, Michael 51–3
Bedau, H. A. 59 n.
benefits, equality of 72–3, 79, 81, 88,
    101, 106, 115, 127
Benn, S. I. 57 n., 61 n.
Bentham, Jeremy 139
Berlin, Isaiah 32–4, 41–2, 45–6, 57 n.
Bradley, F. H. 18–19
Burnheim, John 156 n.

Carritt, E. F. 131 n.
Caudwell, Christopher 33, 45, 49
choice 35–41, 44–5, 48–9, 174–5
class 109–10, 120
coercion 36, 40–1, 49, 74–5, 89–91
Cohen, G. A. 153 n.
common culture 124–5
communism 117
community 89–100
compensation 80–2, 86, 115
competition 75–6, 87–8, 102–3, 120
contract, freedom of 25–6, 46–7, 146,
    152
co-operation 69–79, 84, 89–92, 130,
    133, 174–5
Crosland, C. A. R. 102 n.
culture 47–9, 106, 119–26

Dahl, Robert A. 156 n.
decentralization 98, 135, 164–5, 170–1
democracy 41–3, 107–9, 125, 135,
    156–75
desert 80–4, 88
Devlin, Patrick 19–21
Diggers 2–4
diminishing marginal utility 63–5

education 22–5, 30, 48–9, 102, 106,
    119–29, 132–4
Engels, F. 5–6, 30–1, 53–4, 109
envy 64
equal consideration of interests 61–2
equal well-being 101, 105, 127
equality of condition 106

equality of opportunity 101–3, 106,
    120–4
experience 7, 56, 77, 131, 174–5
exploitation 75, 89–91, 97

Factory Acts 22, 25–6, 29–30
Fascism 34
Flew, Antony 134–5
Francis, Leslie Pickering 96 n.
freedom and equality, relation between
    2–5, 55, 74–7, 91–2, 131–54, 160,
    175
Friedman, Milton and Rose 131 n.
fully human life 9–11, 18, 35

Gould, Bryan 131 n.
Green, T. H. 21–2, 26–37, 49–54

happiness 8–10
Hare, R. M. 58 n., 63 n.
harm 14–17
Hayek, F. A. 39, 131 n., 132
Hegel, G. W. F. 18, 30, 52
Hume, David 3–4, 131 n.

ideology 5–7
incentives 82, 84–8, 118, 128
individual and society, relation between
    12–13, 18–21, 50–5, 84, 133,
    151–3

Joseph, Sir Keith 131 n.
jury system 168–71
justice 64–9, 72–3, 79–88, 144–5

Kant, Immanuel 91–2, 145
Kinnock, Neil 131 n.

Landesman, Bruce 81 n., 101 n.
Laslett, P. 59 n.
Letwin, William 131 n.
Lloyd Thomas, David 132 n.
Locke, John 138, 141–2
Lucas, J. R. 155–6

Macpherson, C. B. 156 n.
mandating 165–8
Marx, Karl 5–6, 18, 30–1, 53–4,
    111–19